SHAPING THE FUTURE

OF CATECHESIS TOGETHER

Shaping
the Future *of*
Catechesis
TOGETHER

Kathy Hendricks

TWENTY-THIRD
PUBLICATIONS
twentythirdpublications.com

Twenty-Third Publications
One Montauk Avenue, Suite 200
New London, CT 06320
(860) 437-3012 or (800) 321-0411
www.twentythirdpublications.com

Cover photo: ©stock.Adobe.com / wavebreakmediamicro

ISBN: 978-1-62785-700-0
Printed in the U.S.A.

 A division of Bayard, Inc.

CONTENTS

INTRODUCTION

In September 2021, parish and diocesan catechetical leaders were preparing for another uncertain year. Thanks to vaccines and an increase in knowledge about the spread of Covid-19, some were considering a return to in-person catechetical sessions, while others maintained virtual sessions. Even as light was starting to emerge at the end of a long and unsettling pandemic experience, there was no question about the seismic shift occurring in the planning and implementation of catechesis. The prevailing question was "What's next?" What would the future of catechesis look like?

To address these and other questions, Twenty-Third Publications, in conjunction with Pflaum Publications, launched a series of five webinars entitled *Shaping the Future of Catechesis Together*. The first four featured a guest presenter who addressed an aspect of the pandemic's impact on catechetical programs and those who implement them; the final webinar summarized the first four and looked to the future. Here is a summary of the series:

> ***"Going Backward to Go Forward"*** • Spiritual director and former diocesan and parish catechetical leader Bill Miller started the series with a reflective session that drew participants into consideration of hope and joy.

Both, he noted, are essential to moving our catechetical efforts forward.

"Family Connections" • Popular author and gifted catechist Connie Clark noted the importance of attentiveness to the ongoing effects of the pandemic and the need for active listening. Through a process called Guided Conversations, she presented thoughtful and insightful questions for reflection based on the Beatitudes and linked to the Covid experience.

"Catechetical Old School" • Former Parish Catechetical Leader (PCL) and Pastoral Associate, Lee Danesco reminded us of the traditional values that we cannot afford to lose amid changing times. She anchored these in community, simplicity, and tenacity and demonstrated how each one keeps us anchored in a solid catechetical vision.

"If the Tech Fits, Do It" • Speaker, coach, and master teacher for Vibrant Faith Denise Utter offered a helpful exploration of the way parishes pivoted during this time by putting digital tools to creative use. In doing so, she presented exciting new possibilities that we can carry forward in this ministry.

"Moving Forward" • In the final webinar, I took the lead by weaving together the threads from the first four webinars and laying out potential pathways for moving forward with a renewed and invigorated vision for catechesis.

All of the webinars were recorded and can be accessed at the following website: https://youtube.com/play-list?list=PLBQIZq8nlWqvCb1cNPC_URKSzDWJfFnNy. The appendixes at the back of this book are the handouts provided by Bill Miller and Connie Clark for their respective sessions.

The process for each webinar entailed input from the presenter and periodic pauses during which participants posted comments and questions in the chat box. The result was a lively and engaging conversation about the challenges as well as the discoveries, insights, and creative possibilities that arose from the Covid-19 experience. This book is both a compilation of insights from the guest presenters' materials and an expanded look at each of the five topics covered in the webinar series. Selected comments from some of the participants appear as sidebars in each chapter as part of the wisdom of the community. I am deeply grateful to each of the presenters for their insightful presentations as well as to the team at Bayard whose work made the series possible. This includes Therese Ratliff, Dan Smart, David Dziena, Kerry Moriarty, Dave Barocsi, and Olivia Turley. Thanks as well to a great editorial and design team—Heidi Busse, Anne Louis Mahoney, Michelle Gerstel, and Jeff McCall.

As I write this, we are not yet finished with the pandemic and its aftermath. Thus, it will take a long time to digest the effects of the past few years and how we both understood and experienced it. As such, the question remains: What is the future of catechesis? My hope is that this book will contribute to the conversation catechetical leaders, catechists, pastors, Catholic school teachers, and others will continue to have. To that end, each chapter includes questions for personal reflection and/or group discussion. Whether you are reading it on your own or with a group of colleagues and co-catechists, may it draw you further into the question and your role in shaping the future of catechesis as we move forward together.

CHAPTER 1

Onset

"Two men will be out in the field; one will be taken, and one will be left. Two women will be grinding at the mill; one will be taken, and one will be left. Therefore, stay awake! For you do not know on which day your Lord will come."

MATTHEW 24:40–42

"For I know well the plans I have in mind for you...plans for your welfare and not for woe, so as to give you a future of hope. When you call me, and come and pray to me, I will listen to you. When you look for me, you will find me. Yes, when you seek me with all your heart, I will let you find me...and I will change your lot; I will gather you together from all the nations and all the places to which I have banished you...and bring you back to the place from which I have exiled you." **JEREMIAH 29:11–14**

"For you do not know..."

March 2020. I was in the middle of a ten-day trip to Florida where I was scheduled to offer back-to-back parish missions along with a mid-week session for Parish Catechetical Leaders (PCLs). I left my hometown of Castle Rock, Colorado, with stresses that had nothing to do with a looming pandemic. My husband, Ron, had broken his ankle while on a trail run. Given his inability to drive, it was not feasible for him to be alone for such a long period, so we arranged for him to stay with our daughter and her family in the mountain town of Salida—a three-hour drive from our house.

The first parish mission took place without disruption, even though news of a pandemic was starting to gain momentum. At the weekend Masses, the pastor invited parishioners to follow the procedures with which they felt most comfortable when it came to sharing the Sign of Peace or receiving communion. By the time of my mid-week presentation to the PCLs, the news was becoming more dire. I am not a sports fan, but the cancellation of the season by the National Basketball Association drew my attention. So, too, did a text from my daughter, warning me of the danger of being away and urging me to return home as quickly as possible. The governor of Colorado had ordered the ski resorts closed, and the situation was clearly becoming serious. It was quickly determined that the second parish mission needed to be cancelled, and I booked a flight home. By the time I reached Salida to fetch Ron, the need to remain with our daughter's family was evident. Not only was it safer for Ron and me, but we were also needed to help care for our two-year-old granddaughter while her parents worked from home.

While these were certainly not the end times foretold in Matthew's gospel, the onset of the pandemic caught us by surprise. Our story was not unique. How many others experienced a similar upheaval of their lives—at home and at work, in their relationships and routines? The isolation and restrictions imposed by the pandemic resulted in an exile of sorts. The impact was enormous. Community life was cut off or curtailed. Schools closed and health systems became overloaded. Layoffs and business closings multiplied. Fear, uncertainty, and stress levels skyrocketed. We were thrust into a time of global "not knowing," seemingly overnight.

FOR REFLECTION OR DISCUSSION

How did your life change because of the pandemic—personally, professionally, and ministerially?

Catechetical Challenges and Opportunities

Parishes, of course, were not exempt from the turmoil. As church doors closed, online possibilities opened. Pastors, PCLs, and others who considered themselves digitally challenged were given crash courses in streaming, online classes, and other virtual offerings. The need to pivot was essential. In the webinar that kicked off the *Shaping the Future of Catechesis Together* series, Bill Miller invited participants to list the ways in which they felt challenged as well as how they experienced new possibilities. In drawing up his own list of challenges, he included the following:

- While the virus proved deadly and contagious, there was also a threat to the mental, emotional, and spiritual well-being of populations in countries across the globe.

> One challenge was apathy. Parishioners who were already marginally engaged stepped away, and the draw to pull them back in isn't there.

- Educating children, youth, and adults was difficult as virtual learning replaced in-person sessions. While the Internet provided creative possibilities, there was a price to be paid for the lack of face-to-face interaction.

- Massive unemployment set off a chain reaction, with short- and long-term damage to both households and entire industries.

- The pandemic uncovered the huge disparities between wealthy nations and poorer ones and exposed weaknesses in our educational, medical, and governmental systems.

- Many people, especially parents, had very limited time for prayer and spiritual reading due to overloaded schedules.

FOR REFLECTION OR DISCUSSION

What would you add to this list?

Possibilities arose during this time as well. Miller listed several that continue to offer potential for a promising catechetical future:

- The effort to research and manufacture a vaccine and make it accessible. In addition to making the reopening of parish life possible, there is hope embedded in such a massive cooperative effort.

- The use of Zoom and other online platforms enabled participation despite the closure of parishes for liturgy and for catechetical programs. In some cases, it provided access for those who were disconnected from parish life prior to the pandemic.

Sharing success stories, I think that as we return to what we did before, we also recognize what doesn't work. Sharing out-of-the-box solutions that are working will bring the Church back together in new ways through worship, catechesis, outreach, and other means. Our needs are different now than before.

- Online programs shifted the responsibility for catechesis more toward parents. This is in keeping with catechetical documents that name parents as primary in the faith formation of their children and families.

- Creativity in lesson planning and resource gathering multiplied as new approaches were tried and tested.

- While some felt the impact of social isolation, in some cases the decrease in outside activity gave rise to more possibility for prayer and reflection.

FOR REFLECTION OR DISCUSSION

What would you add to this list?

What's Next?

"People do not put new wine into old wineskins. Otherwise the skins burst, the wine spills out, and the skins are ruined. Rather, they pour new wine into fresh wineskins, and both are preserved."
MATTHEW 9:17

The impact of Covid-19 on catechesis will take much more time to be understood and processed. Thus, we will continue to add to the lists of challenges and possibilities as the aftermath of the pandemic unfolds. What is clear at this early stage, however, is that we cannot move backward. Nor can we ignore the enormous changes that we underwent as a global and national community and as a church. There is no returning to the way it used to be, no matter how tempting "getting back to normal" sounds. The fact is, we are on the brink of a new normal. What is needed is both new wine *and* new wineskins. As a way forward, I suggest a *CCD approach* that focuses on three primary aspects of catechesis:

- *Catechist:* Expanding and honoring the threefold identity of the catechist as named in the *Directory for Catechesis*, along with taking new approaches to formational processes and experiences;

- *Content:* Revitalizing the message of catechesis in light of new realities, challenges, potential, and possibilities;

- *Dynamics:* Making use of new technologies while holding onto traditional approaches that are at the heart of solid and well-grounded catechesis.

> The pandemic left many people feeling "unseen" in their isolation. Breaking that cycle of isolation—starting with leaders reaching out to catechetical ministers—would help us feel "seen" in our ministry. And on our part: reaching out to others where they are, not where we imagine them to be.

In the next three chapters, I will look at each one of these aspects. In doing so, I will draw upon the webinar series and expand upon the ideas and insights that arose from them.

FOR REFLECTION OR DISCUSSION

What do you regard as the "next step" in catechesis? What new wine and new wineskins do we need to move forward?

CHAPTER 2

Catechist Identity and Formation

On 23rd March 2020 Pope Francis approved the new
Directory for Catechesis *which we have the honor
and the responsibility of presenting to the Church.
It represents a further stage in the dynamic renewal
that catechesis carries out.* **PREFACE, DIRECTORY FOR CATECHESIS**

*Worthy of praise too is that army of catechists, both men
and women, to whom missionary work among the nations
is so indebted, who imbued with an apostolic spirit make an
outstanding and absolutely necessary contribution to the
spread of the faith and the Church by their great work. In
our days, when there are so few clerics to evangelize such
great multitudes and to carry out the pastoral ministry, the
role of catechists is of the highest importance.*

ANTIQUUM MINISTERIUM: INSTITUTING THE MINISTRY OF THE CATECHIST

While the pandemic continued to unfold, two major events took place that presaged hope for the catechetical community. The first was the release of the new *Directory for Catechesis* (DC), a document that offers a next step in the catechetical renewal that has been taking place since the closure of the Second Vatican Council in 1965. Built upon previous catechetical documents, including the *General Directory for Catechesis* and *Catechesi Tradendae*, the *Directory* makes the connection between catechesis and evangelization a key feature. The document underscores Pope Francis' emphasis on encounter and accompaniment. This entails a person-to-person approach— one that is warm, welcoming, and inclusive. This makes the role and responsibility of the catechist a top priority.

It also gives rise to the second major event—the release of the Apostolic Letter *Antiquum Ministerium*. In this short but important document, Pope Francis formally established the lay ministry of the catechist. Not only does this acknowledge and affirm the role that lay catechists have played in spreading the faith, but it also announces a forthcoming "Rite of Institution of the lay ministry of Catechist." While catechists have been recognized and affirmed through events like Catechetical Sunday, the pope's announcement furthers the recognition of the catechist as a vital minister in the church's mission of evangelization.

Both documents emphasize the importance of catechist formation. The Preface for the *Directory for Catechesis* notes how a significant amount of attention has been given to the formation of the catechist because "only catechists who live out their ministry as a vocation can contribute to the efficacy of catechesis." *Antiquum Ministerium* calls upon Episcopal Conferences to determine the kinds of formation catechists will need as they carry out their ministry in an effective and appropriate manner. Such renewed emphasis on the person of the catechist will call for a revitalized approach to catechist formation.

There is still much to unpack in both documents but each one underscores the importance of a catechetical vision that is inclusive, hopeful, inspirational, healing, and forward looking. As a way to provide catechists, catechetical leaders, pastors, and parents with an introduction to the *Directory for Catechesis*, Twenty-Third Publications released a series called *Refresh Your Faith*. It consists of three booklets, each focused on a different aspect of and way to apply the principles of the *Directory*. A fourth component is a digital asset aimed at the "casual catechesis" that takes place in the home. (You will find a listing of the series on the Resources page at the end of this book.) I was given the opportunity to write the booklet on *The Holiness of the Catechist*. In making my way through the *Directory*, I was taken with the description of the catechist's "threefold identity." It certainly provided rich material for considering the holiness of the catechist. As I continue to reflect on this passage, I also see rich potential for new forms and models of formation for catechists—ones that assist in shap-

> I think formation needs to be focused on having an encounter with Jesus so that we can help others with meeting Jesus.

ing the role and responsibility for teaching and sharing the faith with others. It must begin, however, with the initial call to being a catechist as an agent of evangelization.

The Call of the Catechist

The catechist is a Christian who receives a particular calling from God that, when accepted in faith, empowers [the catechist] for the service of the transmission of faith and for the task of initiating others into the Christian life. DC, 112

In one of my first jobs as a parish catechetical leader (PCL), I struggled with the task of finding catechists for each grade. The small Alaskan community in which I worked made for a limited pool of volunteers to call upon. After repeated failures in finding someone to teach the fifth-grade class, I resorted to a last-ditch plea with a pulpit announcement. As the congregation dispersed, a parishioner approached me with what I thought was an offer to volunteer. Instead, he told me how desperate I seemed and then wished me good luck before walking away. It was a brutal reminder of how *not* to recruit catechists. In hindsight, I also see that my approach not only looked desperate and rather pathetic but also diminished the call of the catechist. If we are only looking for warm bodies to fill a position, then we are flubbing the invitation to vocation.

The *Directory* notes that the reasons for answering the call to being a catechist may vary but that each one is a means through which God calls the entire church into service. This makes the catechist an active participant in the missionary discipleship that is at the heart of the church's activity. The Holy Spirit ignites and inspires all of catechesis, and so we are each nurtured in our call by this Divine force.

This understanding will necessarily lead us less to *recruiting* catechists and more to helping them *discern* this call. It may well be that a bulletin or pulpit announcement spurs someone to respond, but discernment takes more time and intention. In my own experience, I went into teaching elementary school with a desire to include religious education as part of my role and responsibility. Thus, I chose to teach in Catholic schools, starting with a three-year commitment in a mission program based in the Diocese of Prince George, British Columbia. An experience of capturing the attention of a group of restless third and fourth graders with a gospel account awakened something in me. I knew this was something I wanted to pursue in depth. As with many lay women and men, it led me along different paths, each of which opened to new and ever-deepening involvement in catechetical leadership, pastoral ministry, writing, and spiritual direction.

The word "vocation" comes from the Latin word for "voice." As the educator Parker Palmer writes, vocation is not a goal to be pursued but a calling to be heard. In his book *Let Your Life Speak*, he notes how our view of vocation becomes distorted when it emanates from an external voice. "Vocation does not come from a voice 'out there' calling me to be something I am not. It comes from a voice 'in here' calling me to be the person I was born to be, to fulfill the original selfhood given me at birth by God." If we are to take seriously the call to the vocation of catechist, we must ground our formational efforts in helping others listen to and answer that call.

This isn't going to take place in a single meeting or after answering a plea from the pulpit. Neither is it going to require a lengthy period of discernment. Most of us no doubt entered the ministry of catechesis in a much less formal way. Even so, our formational approaches need to include an ongoing process of listening to the internal voice that empowers us to become effective witnesses, teachers, educators, mystagogues, accompaniers, and keepers of the memory of God: in short, to recognize and live out our threefold identity as catechists.

What does this mean in terms of catechist formation? The spiritual writer Henri Nouwen once observed our tendency to tie ministry to work *"for* people *by* people." This is a fine way to describe the kind of service that ministers provide. To recognize the calling that lies beneath the ministry, however, we need to go deeper. Thus, Nouwen drew a connection between the call to ministry and contemplation.

> Contemplation enables us to see the gifts in those to whom we minister. And ministry is first of all, the reception and affirmation of what we hear sounding through them, so that they themselves may recognize their own giftedness. What more beautiful ministry is there than the ministry by which we make others aware of the love, truth, and beauty they reveal to us. **QUOTED IN MICHAEL SCHUT,**
> **ED. SIMPLER LIVING, COMPASSIONATE LIFE**

This connects beautifully with Palmer's observation about the need to listen to one's inner voice as a way to discern one's vocation. It makes the process of discernment a starting point for catechist formation—one that invites the catechist to name, reflect upon, and embrace their essential giftedness. Palmer notes that our strongest gifts are those of which we are barely aware. They are part of our nature and thus flow easily. This makes the vocation of the catechist both universal as well as unique; it varies from one person to the next. At a skills level, the individual gifts of a catechist contribute to the larger enterprise of catechesis. While some are highly imaginative when it comes to the fine arts, others are adept at making theological concepts understandable to young minds. What I experienced with the third and fourth graders was an ability to bring Scripture alive for them in a creative and engaging way. It sprang from a deep desire to share the merciful message that I cherish in the Bible, particularly the teachings, ministry, and healing work of Jesus.

Spiritual gifts are a bit trickier to identity. They are deeply ingrained in our nature: mercy, kindness, understanding, wisdom, patience, and fortitude, to name a few. These innate gifts animate the ministry of catechesis and make it authentic. Consider the catechist who has the natural ability to empathize with her learners or the one who models hospitality and inclusion. While catechetical leaders often desire volunteers with particular skills to carry out programmatic needs, it is equally important to seek out those with the gifts that contribute to the essential *ministry* of catechesis. How, then, does this fit into formational efforts?

When speaking to catechists over the years, I often share a story I found in *Christian Century* magazine. It is about a man named Red who, after retiring from a prestigious position in a local business, volunteers at his church as a preschool Sunday school teacher. The image of a successful businessman sitting on the floor and sharing Bible stories with little children is striking. What emerges is his innate gifts of gentleness, kindness, and hospitality. In every instance, the story offered the catechists a renewed appreciation for and understanding of spiritual gifts. They could easily recognize Red's gifts and then make a connection with their own. There are formal ways, such as spiritual gift inventories and other tools, to do this, but the use of a story has great impact. Whatever the means, the inclusion of spiritual gifts as part of the call to vocation is vital to the formation process. In doing so, we lay the groundwork for understanding the connection between catechesis and evangelization.

> Jesus calls us all to spread the gospel. How is the catechist's call unique and separate from all other Christians' in the mission to spread the gospel? Does this uniqueness tell us who will make a good catechist, or are there other traits we should look for?

FOR REFLECTION OR DISCUSSION

Call to mind your own experience. When did you first "get the call" to be a catechist? Perhaps it was a literal call from a catechetical leader or a stirring in you when those announcements were made from the pulpit or the bulletin. What keeps you answering that call?

The Catechist as an Agent of Evangelization

Evangelizing is not, in the first place, the delivery of a doctrine;
but rather, making present and announcing Jesus Christ. DC, 29

Poll a group of Catholics around their image of evangelization and you are likely to hear responses associated with soapboxes, doorbell ringers, and TV preachers. While we have been talking about the "new evangelization" for decades, old associations persist. Nevertheless, the *Directory for Catechesis*, like its predecessors, makes an emphatic connection between evangelization and catechesis. One clear need in the formation of catechists is to develop a more cogent understanding of evangelization and a deeper recognition of their role in it.

A striking image of evangelization appears in the Acts of the Apostles when the disciples—fresh from their Pentecost experience—rush out of the upper room to share the message of Jesus Christ with others. Their initial enthusiasm, along with the more sustained role of carrying out the mission of the gospel, is enflamed by the Holy Spirit. The scene that follows offers a glimpse into the same evangelizing spirit that must accompany catechesis:

> [T]hey gathered in a large crowd, but they were confused because each one heard them speaking in his own language. They were astounded, and in amazement they asked, "Are not all these people who are speaking Galileans? Then how does each of us hear them in his own native language?" ACTS 2:6–8

Read within the context of the evangelization efforts of catechists, this passage means more than becoming instantly multilingual. In a more expansive interpretation, we recognize the call to share the faith *in our own way*. In his Apostolic Exhortation *Evangelii Gaudium*, Pope Francis emphasizes the importance of rediscovering and sharing the gospel with ingenuity and imagination. "Whenever we make the effort to return to the source and to recover the original freshness of the Gospel, new avenues arise, new paths of creativity open up, with different forms of expression, more eloquent signs and words with new meaning for today's world. Every form of authentic evangelization is always 'new'" (11). This requires staying open and attentive to the "original freshness" of the gospel.

In his webinar that opened the *Shaping the Future of Catechesis Together* series, Bill Miller emphasized the need for hope and joy as part of our catechetical efforts. In doing so, he raised some thoughtful questions: *In difficult times such as these, where do you find hope? What strengthens your ability to hope?* Responses from participants poured into the chat box, including these:

- I find hope in the Holy Spirit and the foundation of the church. We have survived this long, and the church will be here long after I am gone.

- Paradoxically, the pandemic itself has provided me more time to increase my prayer time, which is a such a source of hope.

- Being with my religious community.

- I find hope in the network of people who gathered online from beyond my parish boundaries… and the fact that, through them, I've connected to many more people.

- I have found myself looking back through history [to events] like the bubonic plague, the persecution of Christians in the early church, and right through to today and how the church has survived, and I have found people that I minister with in my diocese find hope in that. This is not a new thing, just another thing.

These responses describe a sense of both the continuity of the Church over time and the here-and-now relationships that bring hope and, along with it, joy. If catechists are not, first and foremost, filled with hope and joy, the message they bring will be sour from the start. It is important to distinguish hope from optimism, wishful thinking, or a last-ditch effort when all else fails. Hope doesn't turn away from everyday realities or become an easy platitude to dismiss anything puzzling, distressing, or frightful. "Hope is not a feeling; it is a decision. And the decision for hope is based on what you believe at the deepest levels— what your most basic convictions are about the world and what the future holds—all based on your faith. You choose hope, not as a naïve wish, but as a choice, with your eyes wide open to the reality of the world" (Jim Wallis, *God's Politics*).

This makes the symbol of hope—the anchor—all the more appropriate. Rather than weighing us down, it grounds us so that we can take a longer view—beyond the fears and the disruption and the seeming hopelessness of a world hell-bent on violence, greed, avarice, power, and exploitation of the meek and the vulnerable. For catechists who rarely see the effects of their evangelizing efforts, hope is a necessity. In the end, it enables them to recognize their place in a much larger process—one that has been going on for millennia, starting with those early enthusiastic disciples.

In like manner, catechetical efforts need to be underscored with joy. In describing the third stage of evangelization—that of sharing the gospel with those who do not know or who reject Jesus—the *Directory* describes evangelizers as "[those] who wish to share their joy, who point to a horizon of beauty and who invite others to a delicious banquet. It is not by proselytizing that the Church grows, but 'by attraction'" (41).

> [We need to] help our catechists see the "big picture" of the relationship of evangelization to catechesis, as well as [take] a realistic look at the contemporary context. Then help them to be firmly grounded in a relationship with Jesus.

Picture the figures from the gospels who took the Good News outward: the woman at the well; those experiencing physical, mental, and emotional healing; the well fed who witnessed a miraculous distribution of bread and fish. Can't you see their enthusiasm—their on-fire urgency to tell others about Jesus? Do we have a similar fire burning in us as we tell the gospel stories, as we explore questions of faith, as we witness to the ways God's love has moved in our lives? Catechists are called not to entertain but to *engage*—to invite others to see and hear and open their minds and hearts to truly good news. In doing so, how joyful do we appear in sharing the Good News? What brings us joy in our faith? How do we witness what it means to be committed to Christ? These are good questions for catechetical leaders to both ponder and draw into their formational efforts with catechists. They also lead to a deeper reflection on the identity of the catechist.

FOR REFLECTION OR DISCUSSION

How do you define evangelization? In what way do you see catechists as agents of evangelization?

The Threefold Identity of the Catechist

One of the most vital parts of the *Directory for Catechesis* is the description of the catechist's call and the threefold identity of the catechist (113). These descriptors—witness and keeper of the memory of God; teacher and mystagogue; accompanier and educator—call for new forms and models of formation that honor this identity and prepare catechists for their ministry. Although it is encapsulated in just a few sections of the document, the threefold identity of the catechist holds rich potential for drawing catechists into a deeper recognition of their roles and responsibilities. As such, it offers renewed potential for the formation of the catechist.

Witness and Keeper of the Memory of God

In experiencing the goodness and truth of the Gospel, in his encounter with the person of Jesus, the catechist keeps, nourishes, and bears witness to the new life that stems from this, and becomes a sign for others. DC, 113

Just as the word "evangelization" can sound intimidating to the average catechist so, too, can the call to *witness*. Witnessing to our faith sounds like something set aside for the great saints and mystics. In truth, the day-to-day practice of inclusion, authenticity, empathy, generosity, kindness, and other ways of following Christ are the most effective forms of witness. After all, no one is going to follow someone who is boring, judgmental, or an obvious hypocrite. That's why the starting point for effective catechesis is the one who witnesses more by example than through words. Looping back to the reflection on spiritual gifts, catechist formation can begin with a recollection of someone who served as a witness of faith and how they did so. Drawing catechists together to share their experiences opens a new appreciation for witness and how it often occurs with little fanfare or apparent notice.

In her webinar, "Catechesis Old School," Lee Danesco related an early experience as a catechetical leader in which she and others responded to a plea for help from two religious sisters who were faltering in their efforts to revitalize a parish catechetical program. This led to a gathering of catechetical leaders that benefited everyone involved. As Danesco described it, "Yes, we definitely wanted to help the sisters, but we were also strongly motivated by the recognition that we were learning from one another." Anyone who has been part of a similar gathering knows how much catechists and catechetical leaders savor the experience of sharing ideas and resources. What keeps such groups together, however, is the witness they provide to one another.

I could relate to Lee's experience by recalling my early efforts as a Director of Religious Education (DRE). Knowing little about the "womb-to-tomb" ministry for which I was responsible—including not knowing what "RCIA" stood for!—I was eager to learn from other, more experienced leaders. Such connections multiplied with the different roles I assumed, from parish to diocese to national catechetical consultant. Not only was I given vital assistance in learning the basics of catechetics, but I also received tremendous inspiration from the dedication, faith, and compassion of those I came to know. This makes the "old school" technique of creating community a vital part of catechist formation, no matter the size or makeup of a parish or diocese. Shared experiences inspire the kind of witness that is essential to passing on the faith.

This, in turn, opens the door to the second descriptor: *keeper of the memory of God*. "Keeping this memory, reawakening it in others, and placing it at the service of the proclamation is the specific vocation of the catechist. The testimony of [the catechist's] life is necessary for the credibility of the mission" (DC, 113). Notice that last line: giving testimony through one's life. This is simply sharing our own story with others. To do this, catechists must cultivate a practice of self-reflection and an openness of the heart. When we fall in love with the word of God, we transmit—or echo—it through the way we proclaim and share it with others. Prayerful practices such as *lectio divina* and Ignatian spirituality are two methods of drawing more deeply into Scripture and making a connection with our lives. When introduced to catechists as part of their formational experience, they become more comfortable using them with their learners.

FOR REFLECTION OR DISCUSSION

Who has served as a witness of faith in your life? What did they do or say that drew you to follow their example?

Teacher and Mystagogue

The catechist has the twofold task of transmitting the content of the faith and leading others into the mystery of faith itself. DC, 113

Jesus turned and saw them following him and said to them, "What are you looking for?" They said to him, "Rabbi" (which translated means Teacher), "where are you staying?" JOHN 1:38

The opening of John's gospel provides a wonderful illustration of Jesus as a master teacher. After being trailed by a pair of John's disciples, Jesus asks a question—the first of many as he schools the disciples in learning and following his teachings. The question itself is what a masterful teacher asks of students: What are you looking for? In using the title "Rabbi," the disciples, in turn, acknowledge their willingness to take on the role of scholars, seeking to learn from someone who teaches with authority and insight. Having first followed the teachings of John, they are now ready to expand their minds, hearts, and souls. They follow Jesus, seeking to stay within the vast circle of his knowledge and wisdom.

As those who transmit the content of the faith, catechists need different kinds of knowledge. The first is *theoretical knowledge*. After Pentecost, the disciples didn't rush into the world with heads full of their own ideas and opinions. They underwent serious formation during their time with Jesus. Thus, in speaking with authority, they were grounded in a knowledge of Jesus' teachings. In like manner, catechists need to know what the church teaches, believes, and practices; how we celebrate through worship and the sacraments; a sense of church history and its institutional structure; and an understanding of Scripture through study of its context and literary genre. Such knowledge doesn't come all at once, of course, but is acquired—like that of disciples—through ongoing learning and reflection. The formation of catechists will entail ongoing educational opportunities to support, affirm, and increase knowledge.

There is also a need for *pastoral knowledge* that keeps us attuned to our inner longings. Understood as part of the language of the heart. Jesus asks the disciples to consider what they are seeking beyond head knowledge. Answering the call of the catechist involves reiterating this same question and then seeking out the essential knowledge that comes through regular practices of prayer, reflection, rest, and replenishment of heart and soul.

As a master teacher, Jesus often answered questions with more questions. He was adept in inviting others to ponder, to consider deeper realities. He knew that the opposite of faith was not doubt but certainty. Catechists as teachers aren't experts; thus the juxtaposition with the *mystagogue*, one who helps others break open the "mystery of our faith." How does one describe, for example, the Holy Spirit? How to adequately encapsulate the experience of being in communion with one another? How to draw out the deepest meaning of Jesus as the water, the bread, the very sustenance of life? How to explain the expansive nature of the reign of God, which is already here and "not yet"?

Jesus taught with parables. He used stories rich in symbolism and yet drawn from everyday experiences that his listeners could understand: planting seeds and harvesting crops, tending sheep and overseeing the growth of a vineyard, searching high and low for a lost coin and awaiting the return of a long-lost son. Seasoned catechists know that there is less of a need to explain than to intrigue, to allow some questions to remain unanswered, and to invite learners to make use of their intuition and imagination as well as their intellect and ability to reason.

There is a wonderful story about a rabbinical student approaching his teacher and asking: "Why does Scripture say 'I will place my Word *on* your heart? Shouldn't it read, 'I will place my Word *in* your heart?'" The rabbi responds that the wording was just as it should be. "The Word is placed on the heart until the heart is softened enough to receive it. Then the Word will fall *into* the heart."

This story has two key points that connect with the formation of catechists. One has to do with the place of contemplation in the ministry of the catechist. In contemplating the Scriptures through practices such as *lectio divina* and centering prayer, the catechist learns to let the word of God settle and fall into the heart. The second is how the rabbi's explanation models the meaning of mystagogy—an embrace of the unknown. In allowing time for our hearts to soften enough to receive the word of God, we open ourselves to mystery and the beauty of not-knowing.

FOR REFLECTION OR DISCUSSION

What kinds of knowledge are essential for being a teacher? How have you come to understand the "mystery of faith" through opening your heart?

Accompanier and Educator

The catechist is an expert in the art of accompaniment, has educational expertise, is able to listen and enter into the dynamics of human growth, becomes a travelling companion with patience and a sense of gradualness, in docility to the action of the Spirit and through a process of formation helps [others] to mature in the Christian life and journey toward God. The catechist, an expert in humanity, knows the joys and hopes of human beings, their sadness and distress and is able to situate them in relation to the Gospel of Jesus. DC, 113

Note the *Directory*'s reference to the catechist as "an expert in humanity." This doesn't mean having an advanced degree in any of the social sciences; rather, it calls for sensitivity toward being human. Once again, Jesus serves as an excellent guide. Consider how he listened to others, how he touched them as he healed their physical and emotional wounds, how he asked questions and didn't assume he knew how they would respond. One of the most beautiful examples of the latter is the account of a blind man named Bartimaeus (Mark 10:46–52). After trying to get Jesus' attention and being shushed by those around him, Bartimaeus is recognized, listened to, and healed. In this account, Jesus models three traits that guide us toward a deeper understanding of what it means to be an expert in humanity.

The first is the *personal attention* he gives to Bartimaeus. Despite the presence of a large crowd, Jesus hears and attends to the one voice among many. In like manner, catechists must be attuned to each individual in their care. Reference to accompaniment occurs over two dozen times in the *Directory*. It's reflective of the emphasis Pope Francis places on the personal interaction that is part of the Christian call. As such, it is a vital part of the identity of the catechist. This style of accompaniment becomes evident in the willingness to walk alongside others, listen to their questions, and allow oneself to be touched by their experiences (DC, 135). Just as Jesus listened attentively to Bartimaeus, so the catechist is called to walk alongside others with compassion, openness, and generosity.

The second is *inclusivity*. It is striking to see how many times Jesus ignores those who think they know what is best for him by restricting those with access to him. It's as if he had his own Secret Service contingent who were tasked with protecting him from the riffraff. Jesus wasn't having it—he never does—and continues to make his ministry inclusive and expansive. At a time when one's infirmities were seen as a sign of one's own (or one's ancestor's) sin, he refused to shun others because of their physical disabilities, social standing, economic, religious, or ethnic status, gender or any other cultural or social construct. The *Directory*'s naming of the catechist as "an expert in humanity" can only be understood in terms of relationship and radical love. Accompaniment requires a recognition of the joys and sorrows, the comforts and distress of others, no matter who they are or where they come from.

The third trait is *attentiveness*. Bartimaeus' need seems obvious, and yet Jesus asks a question oriented toward service and caring: "What do you want me to do for you?" This is an apt question for catechists to ask and an essential part of accompanying others in their walk of faith. It's way too easy to assume we know what others need. To be both an effective educator and an artful accompanier, a catechist must be adept in listening to both the spoken and the unspoken needs, desires, and longings of those in their care.

> We need to meet [catechists] where they are at. They are not stay-at-home moms anymore. They are stretched thin.

Catechesis is very much a well-rounded experience—one that is holistic and integrated with life. The Catholic understanding of sacramentality underscores this as we recognize the way in which God's presence is imbued in the world around us. In her book *Understanding the Sacraments*, Barbara Radtke notes how sacramentality is the fabric of our lives. "Rather than removing ourselves or looking away from the world, a sacramental view of life encourages us to look at the world, at all that has been created, for signs of God's presence in its midst." This makes the coupling of educator with accompanier so natural. When we walk alongside those in our care, we can discover the view together.

FOR REFLECTION OR DISCUSSION

How are you continuing to learn what it means to be truly human? Who are you accompanying on their path of faith?

As we move forward in our ministry, the catechist's call entails a revitalized look at what we are bringing to others so that the Good News remains vibrant and relevant to these challenging times.

CHAPTER 3

Content: Sharing the Good News

> *Christ calls each of us, laity and clergy alike, to find*
> *ways to minister to the brokenness of our workplaces,*
> *neighborhoods, or world. The more we enter into the hearts*
> *and dilemmas of others, the more suffering we uncover, and*
> *the more we are wounded by our own compassion for them.*
>
> **RON FARR**

The numbers are staggering. According to the Centers for Disease Control and World Health Organization, as of March 9, 2022:

- The deaths in the U.S. due to Covid-19 topped 959,000, and the total number of cases in the U.S. was close to 80 million.

- Worldwide, the number of cases topped 448 million, with over 6 million dead.

For each death and each confirmed case, there is a circle of other people affected: those who mourn the loss of loved ones; those who have recovered but are dealing with long-term effects; those who have known isolation, fear, and the ongoing strife around issues like vaccines and mask wearing.

The Covid pandemic isn't the only challenge facing us. As I write this, the invasion of Ukraine by Russian forces has captured the world's attention as millions of people flee the country and the conflict escalates. The scourges of racism, homophobia, misogyny, anti-Semitism, and xenophobia continue to undermine human dignity at every level and give rise to increasing physical and verbal violence. Warfare, hunger, and relentless poverty have generated a refugee crisis of epic proportions. The list goes on... If ever there was a time for Good News, this is it.

All of this underscores the challenges we face in catechetical ministry. We cannot carry on as before. The need for the Church to serve as a place of healing and service is more critical than ever. Pope Francis describes what this means:

The thing the church needs most today is the ability to heal wounds and to warm the hearts of the faithful; it needs nearness, proximity. I see the church as a field hospital after battle. It is useless to ask a seriously injured person if he has high cholester-

38

ol and about the level of his blood sugars! You have to heal his wounds. Then we can talk about everything else. Heal the wounds, heal the wounds....And you have to start from the ground up. ***AMERICA,* "A BIG HEART OPEN TO GOD," INTERVIEW WITH ANDREA SPADORO, SJ, SEPTEMBER 30, 2013**

There are many wounds to heal and a great need for warming our collective heart. What we offer through our catechetical efforts is critical.

The Importance of *Good* News

In the previous chapter, we looked at the formation of catechists as key to the forward movement of catechesis. Equally important is the message catechists bring. The first section of the *Catechism of the Catholic Church* focuses on the revelation of God as expressed in the Apostles' Creed as well as the Nicene Creed. In his book *I Believe in God*, Thomas Rausch describes the vitality of the Apostles' Creed when brought to life through active and mature faith.

> For the Christian, the Creed is not just theology. It is the church's confession of faith, rooted in Scripture and the baptismal formularies of the primitive church. The Creed constitutes the church's rule of faith. It can never be a mere statement of opinion...The Apostles' Creed once formed the basis of a solemn commitment made liturgically after several years of catechesis, prayer, and

reflection, the remnants of which we have today in the Rite of Christian Initiation of Adults (RCIA).

How committed and solemn does the typical recitation of the Creed come across at Sunday Mass? How might we revitalize our most basic and cherished beliefs in light of current events and in the aftermath of pandemic challenges? These questions are a critical part of shaping the future of catechesis. As the call to being a catechist is renewed and invigorated, we must also look at the Good News we have to share. Sister Janet Schaeffler notes the importance of drawing upon the Creeds in a way that goes beyond their rote recitation.

> By its very nature, a creed needs to connect our head and our heart. There is a difference between knowing the creed and living it. We are called to transform the ideas and knowledge of the creed into our personal values, into the way we live our lives. ... When we allow ourselves time to think and pray, however, the creed can always be ever new and challenging. *THE CREED: A CATECHIST'S GUIDE*

Consider the great beliefs that are expressed in both the Apostles' and the Nicene Creeds: Trinity, Incarnation, Paschal Mystery, the marks of the church, and the communion of saints. Each one has the potential to bring us to our knees in wonder and draw us further into a rich connection with both everyday life and ever-deepening mystery. While the word "dogma" can sound stodgy and immovable, these basic truths continue to be revelatory and enlightening. As the *Catechism* states: "There is an organic connection between our spiritual life and the dogmas. Dogmas are lights along the path of faith; they illuminate it and make it secure. Conversely, if our life is upright, our intellect and heart will be open to welcome the light shed by the dogmas of faith" (89).

The weight of global events and post-pandemic uncertainty make the essential content of the faith, as shared through evangelization and catechesis, all the more urgent. It also illuminates and offers the kind of healing and hope that Pope Francis described as a critical need in today's world. This content is set forth in the *Catechism of the Catholic Church* and carried through in the publication of solid, age-appropriate catechetical resources. Four elements of this content hold particular relevance as we move forward in our catechetical efforts: Scripture, sacred mystery, works of mercy and justice, and prayer and spiritual practice.

FOR REFLECTION OR DISCUSSION

What dogmas provide a path of light in your life? How does the content of catechesis bring hope and restoration amid global, national, and individual struggles?

Starting with Scripture

As a child, I mostly regarded the Bible as a coffee table book. A huge copy rested in our living room as a decorative element. The only reason to open it was to view the record of family births and deaths listed on its front pages. My mother once valiantly embarked on a mission to read it. After starting with Genesis, she bogged down in the Book of Numbers and then set it down for good. My mother-in-law once told me of her interest in a Scripture study group but then confessed that she didn't know enough about the Bible to join. While the desire was there with both, the idea of exploring the Bible was too daunting.

Happily, an increased comfort with and study of Scripture occurred after the closure of the Second Vatican Council in the 1960s. Scripture studies, lectionary resources, and online courses on various themes and books of the Bible are now readily available. Catechetical texts for children and young people are anchored in accounts from the gospels as well as the salvation stories in the Old Testament. Catechists continue to engage learners in knowing and understanding biblical passages in creative ways. The practice of *lectio divina* and Ignatian spiritual exercises has given rise to the use of Scripture for prayer and meditation.

As part of her webinar on family connections, Connie Clark outlined the process of guided conversation as a framework for sharing. She noted its usefulness in catechesis for drawing families into conversation, especially as they process the impact of the Covid-19 pandemic: "The intention is to guide families toward seeing their experiences in the light of Christ's love." Clark then drew the webinar participants into an example of a guided conversation by drawing upon the Beatitudes from the Gospel of Matthew. Through questions related to the experience of the pandemic, she offers a fresh way to read and reflect upon a familiar gospel and to make a connection with current realities. Here is her example of being poor in spirit:

"Blessed are the poor in spirit, for theirs is the kingdom of heaven."
Questions/Conversation Starters:

- Where was I poor during the pandemic?

- What did I miss most? How were our family celebrations "poor" but truly blessed?

- When was I afraid?

- Where was my understanding "poor"? (Were there events or people I underestimated? When and how did that change?)

- Action item: *Whom do I need to thank?*

Take note of the renewed relevance of an ancient text. Such an approach to Scripture keeps it connected with the difficulties we continue to face and draws us into a deeper reflection on how we might respond in the way of Christ. (See Appendix 3 at the end of this book for the rest of the Beatitude conversation.)

Over the past two years, I offered several presentations via Zoom to catechists, Catholic school teachers, and ministerial leaders about the challenges they faced with the pandemic. In doing so I drew on Scripture as a basis for each presentation. The accounts of Bartimaeus and of Martha and Mary, and the words of the prophet Isaiah about exile, fit beautifully with contemporary struggles around the need for healing, the seeking of "a better part," and the experience of isolation and alienation—all of which were part of the pandemic experience. It goes without saying that Scripture must continue to be a grounding point for catechetical efforts. As we shape the future of the ministry, Scripture will also be a source of tremendous insight and inspiration.

> It occurs to me that one of the things that [the book] *The Chosen* did when it broke into the mainstream is that it allowed the gospel to be freely accessible to all.

FOR REFLECTION OR DISCUSSION

How might your catechetical efforts include a revitalized use of Scripture to guide conversation, increase compassion and understanding, and provide healing and hope? What part of Scripture has given you comfort and revitalized your faith during the Covid-19 pandemic?

Sacred Mystery: Trinity, Incarnation, and Paschal Mystery

There is a story attributed to Saint Augustine in which he was walking along a seashore. He came across a child who was emptying a bucketful of water from the sea into a hole in the sand. When asked what he was attempting to do, the child said he was going to place the entire ocean in the hole. When Augustine noted its impossibility, the child responded by saying it was easier to do than Augustine's attempt at understanding the Trinity. This story constituted an entire year's worth of learning about the mystery of the Trinity when I was in third grade. The message was clear: don't go there!

It's not hard to imagine that many adults have stopped trying to ponder the mystery of "three Persons in one God" because it simply boggles the mind. I suppose I thought so, too, until a friend from college asked me to explain my belief in God. The result was a long handwritten letter in which I described knowing God as simultaneously transcendent, companion, and interior vision. Perhaps I had absorbed more about the trinitarian doctrine than I realized.

Our associations with mysteries generally have to do with solving them, à la Sherlock Holmes. This is a far cry from the meaning of a sacred mystery. In his book *The Divine Dance*, Richard Rohr explains: "Remember, mystery isn't something that you *cannot* understand—it is something that you can *endlessly understand*! There is no point at which you can say, 'I've got it.' Always and forever, mystery gets *you*!" The mystery of all mysteries is the Holy Trinity. As the *Directory for Catechesis* describes it, the Holy Trinity is the "central mystery of Christian faith and life. It is the mystery of God in himself. It is therefore the source of all the other mysteries of faith, the light that enlightens them" (168). So perhaps the story of the child emptying the sea into a hole makes some sense. One can never reach bottom in finding ways to wonder about and ponder the great mystery of God.

From there flows the mystery of the Incarnation, God with us. "And the Word became flesh and made his dwelling among us, and we saw his glory, the glory as of the Father's only Son, full of grace and truth" (John 1:14). Theologian John Shea tells a story about a little girl who is frightened by a thunderstorm. When her mother comforts her by telling her God is near, the child responds, "I know, but right now I need someone with some skin." Don't we all?

Retelling this story in his book *The Holy Longing*, Ronald Rolheiser offers a beautiful explanation of the mystery of the Incarnation:

> We are not angels without bodies, but sensual creatures in the true sense of the word sensuality....God takes on flesh so that every home becomes a church, every child becomes the Christ-child, and all food and drink become a sacrament. God's many faces are now everywhere, in flesh, tempered and turned down, so that our human eyes can see him. God, in his many-faced face, has become as accessible, and visible, as the nearest water tap. That is the why of the incarnation.

The art of accompaniment that is so essential to the ministry of catechesis is wrapped within a larger recognition of being accompanied in our life and faith by Christ who is ever present to us. Once we become aware of this presence, life takes on a different hue. We cannot *not* see God's presence in everyone and everything around us. The great mystic Mechthild of Magdeburg encapsulated this beautifully when she wrote: "The day of my spiritual awakening was the day I saw and knew I saw all things in God and God in all things."

Such vision is clear-eyed about both the joys and the trials in life. The celebration of the Triduum—the high point of the liturgical year—takes us through both the death and the rising of Jesus Christ. The Paschal Mystery is truly one of the most mystifying of our faith, allowing us to embrace the cross without succumbing to despair or desolation. For those who have known deep and devastating loss, the offering of platitudes holds no hope or comfort. Catechesis never bypasses the Paschal Mystery in favor of something lighter and more palatable. Instead, we delve deeply into the mystery of death and the life that can and does emerge from it.

In these three great mysteries of faith, we recognize our essential unity with God and the grace of God's presence within and among us. As so many people have struggled with tragedy, loss, anxiety, depression, and other maladies brought on by the Covid-19 pandemic, our belief in the presence of God offers hope and possibility. As such, the essential content of catechesis remains intact and relevant for present-day realities. The *Directory for Catechesis* acknowledges the unfolding nature of such revelation, howev-

> Jesus was all about relationships. Anything that builds and sustains relationships is solid gold as part of the catechetical effort. We must keep meeting and supporting one another in this important enterprise of catechesis!

er, and calls for "gradualness" in walking the path of faith with others. This requires patience on the part of catechists and catechetical leaders. In her webinar on tried-and-true catechesis, Lee Danesco named the importance of *tenacity*. "Despite personal hardships, roadblocks, and endless anxiety, we continue to gather and reflect, pray, and plan, recruit and train, and do our level best to catechize...We just keep going."

As we shape the future of catechesis, we will continue to share with others the great mystery of God's being, presence, and movement in our lives. As we do so, we must also draw upon the works of mercy and call to justice that are at the heart of active discipleship.

FOR REFLECTION OR DISCUSSION

How do you connect these and other sacred mysteries to the realities of today's world? How might we accompany others as they grapple with questions around God's presence and love?

Works of Mercy

You have been told...what is good, and what the Lord requires of you. Only to do justice and to love goodness, and to walk humbly with your God. MICAH 6:8

Take a moment to slowly read over the following lists of mercy and social action. What words or phrases stand out as particular needs for this time?

The Corporal Works of Mercy

- Feed the hungry
- Give drink to the thirsty
- Shelter the homeless
- Clothe the naked
- Visit the sick and imprisoned
- Bury the dead
- Give alms to the poor

The Spiritual Works of Mercy

- Instruct the ignorant
- Counsel the doubtful
- Admonish the sinner
- Console the sorrowful
- Forgive injuries
- Bear wrongs patiently
- Pray for the living and the dead

The Seven Themes of Catholic Social Teaching

- Life and Dignity of the Human Person
- Call to Family, Community, and Participation
- Rights and Responsibilities
- Option for the Poor and Vulnerable
- The Dignity of Work and the Rights of Workers
- Solidarity
- Care for God's Creation

As Catholics, we are used to the dedication of a year toward a particular theme or call, such as "The Year of the Eucharist" or "The Year of the Family." I don't think one ever took hold in quite the same way as the 2015–16 Year of Mercy. In his declaration for the year, Pope Francis explained its importance: "I have decided to announce an Extraordinary Jubilee which has at its center the mercy of God. It will be a Holy Year of Mercy. We want to live in the light of the word of the Lord: 'Be merciful, even as your Father is merciful.'"

Consider the extreme polarization in our society today. At a time when we should be looking out for one another in a show of solidarity, we are deeply immersed in culture wars, vitriolic political divisions, and the exposure of our racist and xenophobic systems of injustice, indifference, and violence. The need for mercy is ongoing.

An essential aspect of the catechist's role is that of forming others for mission. "Catechesis ... forms believers for mission, accompanying them in the maturation of attitudes of faith and making them aware that they are *missionary disciples*, called to participate actively in the proclamation of the Gospel and to make the Kingdom of God present in the world" (DC, 50). While this is certainly a challenging time in our history, it is also an opportunity to show the best of who we are as believers in Jesus Christ. What better way to do so than by calling others to do what is right (justice), to love goodness, and to walk humbly with God?

One of the people who exemplifies this walk is the Jesuit priest Gregory Boyle, founder of Homeboy Industries. This initiative seeks not only to rehabilitate those involved in gangs and other self-destructive activities but also to instill in them a sense of their intrinsic worth. He describes the work and mission of Homeboy as creating a community of kinship and circle of compassion. "We locate ourselves with the poor and the powerless and the voiceless. At the edges, we join the easily despised and the readily left out. We stand with the demonized so that the demonizing will stop. We situate ourselves right next to the disposable so that the day will come when we stop throwing people away" (*Tattoos on the Heart: The Power of Radical Kinship*).

We have no shortage of saints who exemplify this call to inclusion and compassion. In places as diverse as the Amazon rainforest and the streets of Los Angeles, women and men of faith have answered the call to solidarity, to minister to those on the margins, to care for the gifts of God's creation, to bind up wounds and protect the inherent dignity of each person, to offer food and drink and a simple extension of hospitality to those hungering in body, mind, heart, and soul. At the start of the pandemic, there was an impressive show of support for those doing similar work. Shout-outs were given to those working on the front lines in hospitals and acknowledgments offered to educators trying to stay connected with their students through online classes. As Covid weariness took hold, the tone changed. Mask mandates and vaccination requirements resulted in demonizing those who were lionized a few months earlier. As a result, there has been a massive level of burnout among nurses, teachers, flight attendants, store clerks, restaurant workers, and others tasked with serving the public. In addition, there has been a steady decline in empathy, understanding, respecting the views and needs of others, and holding to the common good.

This situation underscores the need for revitalizing Catholic values around mercy and justice. It is also a time to consider those who are marginalized in our communities and ministerial situations. Who are those we might tend to overlook, ignore, or rebuke? In defining the three dimensions of the Christian life, the *Directory* notes the importance of "charity and witness" along with knowledge of Scripture and participation in the liturgical and sacramental life of the Church. Following the example of the saints, our catechetical efforts must not only include the words of Good News but also the works that accompany them.

> Bishop Barron says that Church teachings on social justice are the cross-generational "glue." We need to use all our resources to share these teachings, but most especially starting with simple things.

FOR REFLECTION OR DISCUSSION

How might we make the call to mercy and justice more integral to catechesis? What do realities in a post-pandemic world call for in terms of catechetical content?

Prayer and Spiritual Practice

There is nothing sadder than a drooping soul.

HILDEGARD OF BINGEN

After decades of speaking to catechists and Catholic school teachers, I learned the importance of including practical, hands-on ideas that hold the attention of students and make for a dynamic lesson. This changed radically during the pandemic. Instead of getting requests to explore more pragmatic topics, I began receiving invitations to address the burnout and spiritual depletion that was becoming more problematic among those working in parishes and schools. Calls for online retreats and sessions oriented toward well-being multiplied. It's clear that the pandemic caused more than a few "drooping souls."

I admit to being heartened by these requests. The importance of a vital spiritual life is no small part of a catechist's call. While writing the booklet on the holiness of the catechist as part of Twenty-Third Publications' *Refresh Your Faith* series, I was struck by the emphasis on holiness in the *Directory*: "It is the herald of a way of life that catechists are also called to follow with constancy and fidelity" (Preface). While the works of catechesis are an essential part of missionary discipleship, so, too, is the development of a rich interior life. The pandemic uncovered the thirst for such a life. As such, future catechetical efforts should include opportunities to share the treasure of spiritual practices that are part of the Church's history and legacy.

Choosing the better part

The Lord said to her in replay, "Martha, Martha, you are anxious
and worried about many things. There is need of only one thing.
Mary has chosen the better part and it will not be taken from her."
LUKE 10:41–42

The account of Martha and Mary in Luke's gospel offers a wonderful juxtaposition of action and contemplation. While Mary's
"better part" can seem to be elevating one over the other, a
careful reading of the text shows something different. Jesus
doesn't comment on what Martha is doing; it's *how* she is
doing it. Entangled in the details of preparing a meal, she lost
any sense of the hospitality that seems to be her innate gift.
"Anxious and worried" could certainly describe how many are
feeling after two-plus years of dealing with a deadly and contagious virus.

This makes the "how-to" of Christian prayer such a needed
element in our catechetical efforts. The fourth section of the
Catechism of the Catholic Church contains a helpful overview
of the forms, expressions, and challenges of prayer. It provides a guide for those seeking to move beyond *saying* prayers
and into a more expansive understanding of *being in* prayer.
We also have the work and reflections of the great mystics to
draw upon. The growing interest in practices like *lectio divina*,
Ignatian exercises, centering prayer, and devotions such as the
Rosary and Eucharistic meditation provide additional possibilities for sharing and expanding an understanding of prayer and
spirituality.

In his Daily Reflection on December 23, 2017, Father Richard Rohr describes prayer as "sitting in the silence until it silences us, choosing gratitude until we are grateful, and praising God until we ourselves are an act of praise" ("Practice: Praying Always"). Such a stance requires the practice of attentiveness and an openness to God's grace. The *Directory* refers to *docibilitas*, a term generally associated with vocational formation, in connection with self-formation. It implies a certain pliability, much like Isaiah's image of wet clay in the hands of the potter, and a willingness to be touched by grace. Applied to prayer and spiritual practice, it makes

> During this time, I've grown in my relationship with the Lord and especially praying for others.

us receptive to the inner peace, gratefulness, and wonder that Rohr describes. Such openness is critical for those involved in shaping the future of catechesis as we are drawn further into the heart of God and back to our own selves.

FOR REFLECTION OR DISCUSSION

What "better part" might we draw upon as we consider our own roles in catechesis? What spiritual needs do you recognize as we move forward in our catechetical efforts?

CHAPTER 4

Dynamics: Shifting Our Approach

After growing frustrated with my clumsy efforts to find the right episode of her favorite TV show, my granddaughter grabbed the remote from my hand and quickly located the correct segment. She is four years old. Her little brother learned to swipe photos on my phone before he learned to walk. The two of them are perfect examples of "digital natives"—those born or brought up during the age of digital technology and therefore familiar with computers and the Internet from an early age. The rest of us qualify as "digital immigrants"—those raised prior to the digital age. These individuals, often Generation X/Xennials and older, did not grow up with computing or the Internet and so have learned to adapt to the new language and practice of digital technologies. For those in parish and catechetical ministry, the onset of the Covid-19 pandemic necessitated a sharp learning curve for the latter.

In her webinar, "If the Tech Fits, Do It," Denise Utter shared examples from several parishes and described how they rose to the challenge. Through streaming services, virtual learning platforms, and various apps, parish leaders managed not only to continue their ministries but also to uncover opportunities for reaching parishioners in new and dynamic ways. Here are just a few of the parish examples from Utter's presentation:

- Digital daily reflections, offered by the pastor on the life and holiness of the saints

- Flocknote to send regular texts and emails as well as welcome messages to new parishioners

- Livestreaming of Sunday Mass using platforms that allow parishioners to greet one another and offer affirmative comments on the prayers, music, and homily

- Livestream of a Saint Patrick's Day cooking demonstration and virtual happy hour

- Parish podcast series featuring interviews with those choosing a new path in life and faith

- Online classes offered through Zoom, GoTo Webinar, and Google Classroom

- Expanded use of social media, such as Facebook, Twitter, and Instagram, to share posts from a Sunday homily and offer affirmations to parents and families

Utter's presentation generated numerous comments throughout the webinar, with ideas around digital media multiplying with each one. It's clear that many parishes met the challenge of pandemic restrictions and continued to carry on their mission. It was also clear that opting out of the digital age was not feasible.

The Ins and Outs of Digital Technology

Increased attention to the possibilities of digital technology did not just arise during the Covid pandemic. Saint John Paul II drew attention to these new technologies in addressing the call for the new evangelization. That means we have been considering their potential for decades. The *Directory for Catechesis* addresses the reality of this technology and the unknowns that are still prevalent around its use:

> The introduction of digital tools and their use on a massive scale has caused profound and complex changes on many levels with cultural, social, and psychological consequences that are not yet entirely evident....The digital, therefore, is not only a part of the existing cultures, but is asserting itself as a new culture: changing language, shaping mentalities, and restructuring value hierarchies. [359]

The document goes on to name the positive attributes of the emerging digital culture. Among these are an expanded capacity for communication as well as access to information and increased knowledge. In writing this book, for example, I have turned multiple times to the Internet to locate additional resources, pull up a quote, or verify a reference. The *Directory* also notes how digital tools extend and enrich human cognitive capacities, such as acquiring, archiving, and retrieving data, which assists in shoring up our collective memory. Consider the adaptive tools now available for those with special needs— from text-to-speech systems to screen-reading software. Such advances make life more inclusive and interactive for those who found themselves left on the margins for way too long.

There are downsides to digital culture as well. The *Directory* notes the potential for exploitation, manipulation, and misinformation. The pandemic provided a radical experience of the latter as misinformation about vaccines, mask wearing, and medical treatment for the virus spread through the Internet. Social media companies have their hands full when it comes to monitoring such misinformation as well as bots, trolls, and a slew of online behavior that promotes hatred, paranoia, fear, and violence. A spiritual downside comes with the loneliness and isolation that results when online relationships replace in-person encounters. "Digital spaces can create a distorted vision of reality, to the point of leading to the neglect of the inner life, visible in the loss of identity and of roots, in cynicism as a response to emptiness, in progressive dehumanization and ever greater isolation within oneself" (DC, 361).

In his 2011 book, *Hamlet's BlackBerry: A Practical Philosophy for Building a Good Life in the Digital Age,* William Powers drew upon similar upsides and downsides to the digital world. "Today we're always just a few taps away from millions of other people, from endless information and stimulation. Family and friends, work and play, news and ideas—sometimes it seems everything we care about has moved to the digital room. So, we spend our days there, living in this new ultra-connected way." It's worth noting that the use of a BlackBerry now needs an explanation for those who came of age since the publication of Powers' book. In fact, he includes a bit of foreshadowing when he writes, "By the time you read this there will be completely new modes of connecting that are all the rage. Our tools are fertile, constantly multiplying."

I learned a lot about technologies that I was not comfortable with and am now a pro.

We could each relate our own positive and negative experiences with the digital culture and its impact on our ministries. The livestreaming of liturgy and catechetical sessions through online platforms allowed parishes to remain in touch with the people they serve. In my own life, I have been able to continue spiritual direction through online visits. I even met a new directee with whom I would not have been able to connect were it not for the Internet. Along with this benefit, however, is a lack of in-person interaction that characterizes the art of accompaniment and is key to both spiritual direction and a catechetical vision.

How do you describe yourself: as a digital native or a digital immigrant? What positive and negative aspects of the digital culture have you witnessed?

The Digital Culture

While the *Directory*'s section on digital technology garnered a great deal of attention, it is important to note its placement within a broader context of culture and interreligious relations. In fact, it is only part of chapter 10, "Catechesis in the Face of Cultural Scenarios." Highlighting the difference between digital natives and digital immigrants, the *Directory* speaks of a larger "anthropological transformation." The approach that digital natives have toward the new technologies and their use entails a different style of discourse. The result is that the digital native is "more spontaneous, interactive, and participatory" (362).

This leads to a different way of learning, accessing information, and relating to others. The *Directory* names three characteristics of this type of learning:

- *A preference for images over listening.* This calls for a new language that is much more visual as well as creative ways for organizing thoughts. Consider the popularity of "vision boards" versus lists to concretize a goal or represent a dream, and well-used sites like Instagram and Pinterest to post photos and share stories.

- **The use of multitasking, hyper textuality, and interactivity.** This results in a more emotional and intuitive way of learning versus the analytical. We are all familiar with the cone of learning that starts with how we remember 10% of what we read and progressing to 90% of what we hear, discuss, and do. While some of that data is now being questioned, the preference for interactive learning cannot be underplayed. Jesus certainly understood this when he sent his disciples—in pairs—to put his teachings into practice.

- **A preference for storytelling over traditional forms of discourse.** "The language that has the greatest hold on the digital generation is that of the story, rather than that of argumentation" (363). This is nothing new. Jesus, after all, used parables to reach not only the mind but also the heart. Catechists need to be adept at telling stories and helping others to do the same.

The *Directory* expands upon these characteristics to also address catechetical challenges in the digital age. The innovation in language, for example, makes one a "consumer and not the decoder of messages." This can render an "anything goes" mentality in which *my* story becomes *the* story. We certainly see this through the rise in pundits who interpret the story for us through a purely subjective lens. Given the rising polarization in our culture, the capacity for empathy, understanding, and compassion gives way to *my* views, *my* rights, and *my* opinions. It also renders truth as malleable to one's own political, religious, or cultural group. Would "alternative facts" be seen as anything but laughable were it not for the power of digital, online, and virtual technology?

The need to move into this technology within catechesis is undeniable. As the *Directory* states: "These horizons show how the digital and its tools are potent means for finding new and unprecedented forms of transmission of the faith, but it is also true that ecclesial action must make known the possible ambiguities of a language that is evocative but hardly communicative of the truth" (364).

Challenges present opportunities. This is something that Powers discusses in his book by noting that every technological change—stretching back to the practices of solitary reading and writing on papyrus—has resulted in resistance as well as opening doors to new and innovative possibilities.

> It's also important to be aware of what is happening in the digital age, especially with older children. How can we connect with them if we aren't aware of what they are immersing themselves in on TV, with movies, games, and TikTok?

The same holds true for catechesis. If the Covid-19 pandemic has shown us anything, it's that we need in-person experiences or, as the *Directory* puts it, "the pain, the fears and the joys of others and the complexity of their personal experiences" (369).

FOR REFLECTION OR DISCUSSION

In what ways are digital technologies opening new avenues for faith formation in the parish and the home? How might catechists and catechetical leaders use digital tools in a manner consistent with catechetical principles and gospel values?

Shifting Our Approach

Several dynamics arose during the pandemic that will have a lasting effect on the future of catechesis. Here are few of them.

The need for pivoting

In writing about the need for urgent and immediate responses during the pandemic, Carole Eipers notes the difference between the parishes that pivoted and those that didn't. Some, she noted, figured the pandemic wouldn't last long and therefore kept their current plans in place, ready for the return to normal that kept getting shelved. Others were paralyzed and made little or no response. The parishes that pivoted faced the same realities but came up with creative responses. "The paralyzed churches focused on the 'way we have done things' rather than why we do them. The pivoting churches asked, 'Why do we do what we do and how can we do it a new way?'" (*Developing a More Flexible Parish: 8 Easy Ways to Practice Pivoting*).

Each of the webinar presenters made similar points. Doing nothing or denying the reality of changes that are here to stay is not sustainable. We must embrace new approaches and creative forms of ministry. Catechists and catechetical leaders not only pivoted toward new ways of organizing and implementing catechetical programs during the pandemic but also recognized the benefits of maintaining some of them in a post-pandemic reality.

Hybrid programs

While some catechists felt out of their league when it came to moving from in-person to online lessons, others found great benefits in doing so. Prior to the onset of the pandemic, I spoke to multiple groups of catechists, catechetical leaders, Catholic school teachers, and pastoral ministers about the challenges of reaching families. When asked about the obstacles they faced, the most frequent response had to do with busy schedules. This affected everything from family attendance at Mass to parents' involvement in the faith formation of their children. It wasn't that parents didn't care; it was that they had so little time to attend to these vital aspects of their children's lives.

Then along came online learning. Several catechists and catechetical leaders noted the ability to reach families who had, for various reasons, ceased to be involved in parish life. Others noted the way in which parents engaged with their child's religious and spiritual formation. More than once, I heard how parishes plan to continue a hybrid approach to their catechetical programming. Doing so allows for options that have otherwise not been considered. It also paves the way for various forms of evangelization.

A *shift in leadership skills*

As Denise Utter wrapped up her presentation on digital catechesis, she noted the shift that was occurring for catechetical leaders. This would entail a new role for the catechetical leader—that of *curator*. We associate the term with museums and art galleries and denotes one who acquires, oversees the care of, and expands a collection. Curators also work in collaboration with other institutions to share materials. In doing so, they work to inform, educate, and inspire the public. Applying these tasks to the catechetical leader, Utter noted the need for a "collection" of digital resources that will facilitate the catechetical mission.

The second aspect of a curator's job—that of collaboration—was emphasized in Lee Danesco's webinar as she related the story of leadership gatherings. With the multiplication of digital resources, the need for such collaboration is key. I recall my own experience and the monthly meetings of DREs organized by our diocesan director. One of my favorite gatherings was the annual viewing of videos for our diocesan library. Situated in a comfortable room at a retreat center and fueled with copious snacks, we spent an entire day watching and deciding upon the films we found useful for sacramental preparation, Scripture study, and age-appropriate catechesis. The cutting-edge technology at that time was the VCR. Now that we have moved to greater access through YouTube, Zoom, Instagram, podcasts, and social media, the possibilities are endless. The role of *master curator* will then fall to leaders in diocesan offices as they not only provide information about various technologies but also draw together parish leaders to discuss, share, and envision their use for catechetical programs.

Facilitation of conversations

Anyone who has been involved in church ministry knows well the potential for conflict that can erupt over everything from paving the parking lot to the appropriate music for a wedding ceremony. Hot-button issues give rise to animosity, and the proliferation of social media and other digital tools elevates the temperature even further. This makes the facilitation of honest and respectful conversation even more important. It is also implied in the threefold identity of the catechist as part of the call to listen and accompany others.

> We need to take an evangelization approach in order to put some of our amazing content into places where they may be bumped into, such as YouTube Kids and Netflix.

In her presentation on guided conversations, Connie Clark noted the synodal process that was opened by Pope Francis and that called for the capacity to listen to one another. To emphasize this point, Clark drew upon the address the Pope gave at the opening of the Synod in October 2021. "The Synod then offers us the opportunity to become a listening Church, to break out of our routine and pause from our pastoral concerns in order to stop and listen."

In chapter 2, I noted the need for catechists to be attentive and adept at listening. This is a major aspect of accompanying others in their walk of faith. Accompaniment plays a large part in the dynamics of catechesis and the shift in our approach to it. As such, it deserves further exploration and consideration as part of these essential dynamics.

....

FOR REFLECTION OR DISCUSSION
....

Which shift in an approach to catechesis do you consider most urgent? What would you add to this list?

An Evangelizing Presence

A key line in the *Directory* names an important dynamic for catechesis: "In the process of proclaiming the Gospel, the real question is not how to use the new technologies to evangelize, but how to become an evangelizing presence on the digital continent" (371). This shifts the emphasis from the tools to the person using them. What does this mean and how do we shift our approach to being an effective catechist within the digital landscape?

If one wanted to encapsulate the papacy of Francis in just a few words, "accompaniment" would be at the top of the list. This dynamic is fleshed out in the new *Directory* with words and phrases such as "proximity," "gratuitousness," "compassion," "respect," and "touched by the questions and situations of life." This can all remain theoretical, however, unless we name some concrete approaches to this evangelizing presence. Here are a few of them.

Offer spaces for experiences of faith

The *Directory* is clear that catechesis cannot simply be dig-italized but must offer spaces for the sharing of one's faith. While online classes and virtual presentations offered creative possibilities during the pandemic, they also created a bit of "Zoom fatigue." The lack of in-person contact took a toll on our physical, mental, and emotional well-being. No matter when or how we choose to use digital technology in the future, its use must include something interactive and personal. Sad to say, some of the examples I saw during the pandemic simply moved the catechist online and into the role of a talking head (sometimes with very poor camera settings!). Digital offerings ought to include time for feedback, discussion, reflection, and other forms of interaction. They also need to be kept shorter—perhaps by chunking content so that participants can take the content into their lives for further reflection and integration.

Facilitate interconnectedness

The *Directory* makes an interesting distinction between person-alizing the process and individualizing it. I mentioned earlier the propensity for personal opinions which, in turn, give rise to a sense of entitlement and self-righteousness. This leads to a lack of regard for the common good. "It is important to help people not to confuse the means with the end, to discern how to navigate online, in such a way as to grow as subjects and not as objects and to go beyond technology in order to recover a humanity renewed in the relationship with Christ" (372).

As I write this, the 2022 invasion of Ukraine is an unfolding tragedy. This horrific situation has sparked an outpouring of support for Ukrainians from around the world and has become a moment of solidarity. The suffering of those whose lives and homes have been destroyed lends much-needed perspective to the sense of entitlement that pervades our lives. More than one social media post has noted the smallness of everyday concerns when placed alongside those who are fleeing their homes or facing death and the devastation wreaked upon their communities. In this and other tragic occurrences, catechesis can invite deeper reflection on the essential bonds that unite us as "one body in Christ" and generate the call to justice and charity that is at the heart of the gospel.

Activate the imagination

The *Directory* uses the liturgy as an example of drawing together various means of interactivity and engaging the senses. It also refers to the use of sacred art to connect people with something larger than themselves. I witnessed the effectiveness of the latter while facilitating a course on Saint Mary Magdalene as part of Boston College's STM Crossroads program. At the beginning of the course, participants were invited to view images of Mary Magdalene. This stimulated conversation and increased participation as the online community began to post additional images. The entire process broadened participants' perceptions of the saint and led to a deeper understanding of her role as disciple and her influence in the early church. Given the highly visual nature of digital natives, the use of art and visual aids is extremely effective.

Invite interior reflection

Asking good questions has long been an important part of effective catechesis. One way to do this is through the "think, write, share" model, which uses questions prior to and after watching a film or other visual presentation. The process invites further reflection and deepens insight. For example: *What are we looking at? What makes you say that? What do you notice (see, feel, know)? What more can we uncover? What do you wonder?* Such an approach removes the catechist from the "front of the class" to a position alongside the learner as accompanier and fellow inquirer.

In our shared blog, "Still Blooming," my friend and collaborator Barbara Radtke wrote an interesting post on the value of cross-generational conversation.

> Online classes allow us to gather families from a large geographic parish, which gives children the sense of being part of a large Catholic community. This supports children who may not have friends or schoolmates that share their faith journey.

She referred to the book *Resurrection Hope: A Future Where Black Lives Matter,* by Kelly Brown Douglas and the conversations the author had—often via text—with her son, Desmond. These centered on questions Desmond was raising about hope, despair, and whether Black lives really did matter in the wake of the 2020 killing of George Floyd. The book and accompanying lecture by Brown Douglas gave rise to a reflection around Radtke's own intergenerational and intercultural conversations. "They are the conversations that began with a stance of openness to learning, of probing the way we framed our questions (often where generational or cultural differences surfaced), and of having patience to keep the conversation open-ended. The process was as important as the conclusion and it was best not to draw the conclusion prematurely." As a mystagogue and accompanier, the catechist is well situated to frame questions that probe a bit deeper and don't reach conclusions too soon.

FOR REFLECTION OR DISCUSSION

How do you define an "agent of evangelization"? In what ways do you see catechists as an evangelizing presence?

As I consider the advances in technology that my grandchildren will see, I am hopeful that these will lead to greater understanding of and empathy for others along with a wider worldview. None of it, however, will overshadow the very human need for connection and interaction, for increased compassion, empathy, and love. This makes the central movement into the future one that is infused with hope and with joy.

CHAPTER 5

Moving Forward with Hope and Joy

So whoever is in Christ is a new creation: the old things have passed away; behold, new things have come. **2 CORINTHIANS 5:17**

Change is inevitable. We may know this intellectually, but the Covid-19 pandemic brought it into full-fledged reality. As my own experience in March 2020 resulted in an overnight change to my life, so did individuals and institutions throughout the world experience this in myriad ways.

The way forward for those in catechetical ministry is in flux, something each of the webinar presenters noted in particular ways:

- In "Catechesis Old School," Lee Danesco noted that it was vital to not do the same thing in the same way over and over again.

- In "If the Tech Fits, Do It," Denise Utter observed that we don't want to go back to old ways of doing things, even if we could.

- In "Family Connections," Connie Clark illustrated how guided conversations remind us of the presence of Christ in the midst of change.

- In "Going Backward to Go Forward," Bill Miller drew upon the challenges of the pandemic to find hope and spread joy in our catechetical efforts.

What struck me about each of these presentations was the way the presenters faced the difficult realities of the pandemic while also offering a hopeful vision of the shape of catechetics for the future. No wonder the number of participants not only remained steady for the entire series but also increased as we moved along.

Hope for the Future

In chapter 2, I noted the reference Bill Miller made to hope and the importance of remaining hopeful despite the challenges we face. Let's expand on this by revisiting the questions posed in the webinar as well as more of the participants' responses.

In difficult times such as these, where do you find hope? What strengthens your ability to hope?

- Our diocese has held bi-weekly check-in meetings for catechetical leaders. This has helped immensely.

- The grace received in the Eucharist strengthens my ability to hope.

- Faith and trusting in God. Being able to attend Mass again and being able to sing in the choir again. Praying.

- Jesus said, let the children come to me. I have been spending a great deal of time with my grandchildren; they have brought me hope that brings me to the Eucharist.

- When I focus on me and/or what is wrong with the world, then I tend to lose hope. When I turn to Christ, when I look to the big picture, then I have hope.

- Being with my religious community.

- I find hope in the network of people who gathered online from beyond my parish boundaries... and the fact that, through them, I've connected to many more people.

- Connecting with others around questions that matter.

- Having the children come back to class!

- Being able to welcome back some of our students in person to PSR [Parish School of Religion] this weekend. I am so excited to be able to see all the children again and to guide them in their faith and celebrate sacraments with them.

- Prayer, reflection on Scripture, praying the Rosary while walking, and the Eucharist (Adoration and Mass), catechizing our children in person.

- I find my hope in prayer and then go out and look for the Holy Spirit working in my life. My hope is strengthened the more I notice the Holy Spirit working.

- I find my hope in the people who now have some spare time to volunteer in programs that are of service to others, such as a food pantry or a childcare center that needs grandparents to provide love to the children.

- Living out the gifts of the Holy Spirit in my daily life gives me immense hope!

FOR REFLECTION OR DISCUSSION

Take a minute to read over this list again. What inspires you about those who posted these comments? What responses do you have to the questions about hope?

In expanding upon the importance of hope, Miller shared excerpts from Pope Benedict's Encyclical *On Christian Hope* (*Spe Salvi*) (see Appendix 1). In doing so, he underscored the importance of moving forward with hope in our catechetical efforts. To do so, it helps to untangle the meaning of hope from some of its misconceptions. I alluded to these in chapter 2 but want to expand on them here.

One misconception is wishful thinking, something that often veils a desire to go back to the way things were. It is a very human reaction. Going backward seems like a safe and secure route. The trouble lies in recalling the past with skewed vision. In his book *Faster: The Acceleration of Just about Everything*, James Gleick calls this "false nostalgia." He notes that the more the present speeds up, the slower we make the past. This happens readily enough in the church when we look back to previous times as idyllic or less uncertain.

Another misconception is mistaking hope for optimism, which can lead to thinking that things will only get better in the future. There is an element of this in hope, to be sure. Sincere hope doesn't mask difficult realities or gloss over suffering, heartache, disappointment, or grief, however. The pandemic gave rise to all of these. As we move forward, our catechetical efforts must address the huge toll taken on individuals, families, and institutions as a deadly virus attacked not only bodies but also minds, hearts, and souls.

The worst of all distortions is seeing hope as a last resort. If a doctor told you, "You have nothing to do now but hope," you can bet your days are numbered. Such thinking is actually the opposite of hope, which holds out for what is possible. The great mystic Julian of Norwich described it as "all will be well, and all will be well, and all manner of things will be well." She didn't indicate that all would be well right now or tomorrow or even in her lifetime. Instead, hope holds to a long-range vision of what will be *in time*. The Czech statesman Vaclav Havel described hope in this way:

> Hope... [is] an ability to work for something because it is good, not just because it stands a chance to succeed. The more unpropitious the situation in which we demonstrate hope, the deeper that hope is. Hope is definitely not the same thing as optimism. It is not the conviction that something will turn out well, but the certainty that something makes sense, regardless of how it turns out.
>
> **DISTURBING THE PEACE**

Brother David Steindl-Rast OSB describes hope as that which "builds God's house"—that uniquely combines "the security of love and the adventure of faith" (*Common Sense Spirituality*). The anchor is an ancient and apt symbol of hope. It is not forever resting at the bottom of the sea but can also be pulled up, allowing the boat to set sail. As such, the anchor symbolizes the necessary balance between drifting and entrenching. Taken to excess, drifting is so open to change that there is no possibility of building anything. On the other hand, extreme entrenching keeps us caught in the past and stifles any semblance of creativity or possibility. Steindl-Rast notes that both are forms of fear in disguise. Hope, however, moves us along with twofold courage: the courage to build and the courage to build lightly. Put another way, hope gives us the boldness to set sail and the sense to seek safe harbor. As so many of the participants in Miller's webinar noted, God's constant presence keeps us anchored. The psalmist describes it beautifully:

My soul, be at rest in God alone, from whom comes my
hope. God alone is my rock and my salvation, my for-
tress; I shall not fall. **PSALM 62:6–7**

Hopeful Agents of Change

To move forward, catechists and catechetical leaders will need
not only to retain hope in their efforts but also to become
hopeful agents of change. Here are four ways of doing this.

Take your place with grace

In "Mighty Trucks of Midnight," Canadian singer/songwriter
Bruce Cockburn uses the image of huge trucks barreling down
a highway to describe the force of change and the way in which
we must give way to the new. In attempting to resist such a
force, we risk getting mowed down. By recognizing the tran-
sience of all things—"all flesh is like grass," as the Bible says (1
Peter 1:24)—we acknowledge that we cannot make things last
forever. Instead, we move forward with grace.

Picture a graceful person. Perhaps it's the image of a dancer
who can pirouette on one toe. Or the smooth movement of a
basketball player who arcs the ball through the air and into the
basket with ease. Synonyms include elegant, supple, nimble,
flowing, and lithe. As grace-filled ministers of the word, catechists possess many of these traits as they draw others into the
knowledge, understanding, appreciation, and practice of their
faith. As "experts in humanity," they do so with compassion,
gentleness, respect, and tenderness. The long-range effects

SHAPING THE FUTURE OF CATECHESIS TOGETHER

of the pandemic have only begun to be recognized and felt. Graceful catechesis for the future will require a great deal of inspiration, guidance, and companionship to help those in our care reflect on experiences of loss, isolation, and stress with authentic hope and trust in the endless grace of God.

Move from certainty to possibility

More than once during the past two years, I heard the pandemic described as the "end times." It's not clear to me why religious people are so eager to see the destruction of the planet. Perhaps it's the desire for certainty. False nostalgia is another possible explanation. Hope doesn't dwell in certainty, however:

> In biblical experience hope draws sustenance not from the predictable, if turbulent, cycles of nature and history but from the God who is Lord of both. Memory and expectation are formed not by the observation that all things come and go but by the conviction that God creates and saves. Indeed, God saves by stepping into the fray of human life and disrupting the course of all the raging waters that sweep us into oblivion. JOHN S. MOGABGAB, "HOPE IN GOD," *WEAVINGS*, VOL. XIV, NO. 6

On January 20, 2021, Amanda Gorman, clad in a bright yellow coat, stepped up to the podium and offered words of hope to a wounded nation. It was inauguration day for President Joseph Biden. Evidence of the insurrection that had taken place on that very spot just two weeks earlier was in clear view. The nation was reeling from the ongoing pandemic, a brutal election and its aftermath of distorted results, and the resurgence of white nationalism. Even so, hope was the undertone of the poet's voice:

> So, while once we asked, how could we possibly prevail over catastrophe, now we assert, how could catastrophe possibly prevail over us?
>
> We will not march back to what was, but move to what shall be: a country that is bruised but whole, benevolent but bold, fierce and free.
>
> We will not be turned around or interrupted by intimidation because we know our inaction and inertia will be the inheritance of the next generation, become the future. **AMANDA GORMAN, "THE HILL WE CLIMB"**

As it goes on, the poem couches certainty within possibility: "But one thing is certain. If we merge mercy with might, and might with right, then love becomes our legacy and change our children's birthright." Gorman's poem, read in its entirety, not only describes the hope abiding in one nation but also throughout the world. As such, it is analogous to the hope-filled possibilities that catechists have to share with a weary world. When our only certainty is of God's everlasting love and mercy, we offer the truest and deepest measure of hope in what we can be.

Practice hospitality

Several years ago, while on a trip to Great Britain, my husband and I stopped at the Hospital of St Cross and Almshouse of Noble Poverty near Winchester. Dating back to the 12th century, it is not, as the name might suggest, a place where sick people were tended but rather a house of hospitality. The roots of our current definition of hospital and hospice—places to tend the sick and the dying—lie in this original meaning. As an almshouse, St Cross was established as a community to help the poor. Today, visitors to the gift shop are offered a piece of bread and small cup of ale as part of the ongoing mission of hospitality.

The practice of hospitality was deeply instilled in people during Jesus' time. In fact, hospitality plays a large part in understanding the post-Resurrection account of the disciples on the road to Emmaus (Luke 24:13–32). *The Jerome Biblical Commentary* notes that it was the invitation to "stay with us" that revealed the presence of Jesus in their midst. "Disciples who entertain the stranger will have their eyes opened." In true evangelizing fashion, the disciples then set off: not to try to find Jesus after he disappeared from their midst but to tell others about this amazing revelation.

I associate hospitality with my mother. When my parents worked with an architect to build our family home, my mother insisted upon enlarging the dining room to accommodate a growing family and to entertain guests. Every time I meet someone who remembers her, they have a story to tell about a meal shared, a party given, or a holiday observed. Our house was filled with laughter, warmth, and lots of food. And my mother oversaw it all.

As part of the Rule he created for his new monastic community, Saint Benedict stressed the importance of welcoming the stranger as one would welcome Christ (Rule of Benedict, Chapter 53). In doing so, he held that every human being is beloved by God and is worthy of respect, dignity, and compassion. In true Benedictine fashion, no one was ever turned away from our family table. All were greeted not as strangers, but—as my father loved to say—as part of our family. It taught me an important lesson about the Eucharistic table. This was one of many personal experiences of the "casual catechesis" that the *Directory* describes as integral to faith formation in the home.

A critical part of receiving another person in such a manner is learning to wait upon him or her with patience. The latter entails service but also attentiveness and an open and listening heart. Such an attitude requires space and time, two commodities that seem to be in short supply in the frenetic pace of our culture. As Jane Tomaine notes in her book *St. Benedict's Toolbox*, "We're often reluctant to take time to be truly present to others, and we can find it difficult to accept people as they are." Hospitality counters these tendencies.

The evangelizing mission of the church brings the Gospel into the world in new and engaging ways. All too often, Christians have used the Bible as a battering ram to hammer people into belief through fear and guilt. Benedict's Rule calls for something far different. As hospitable catechists, we invite rather than coerce. We listen rather than harangue. We take people for who they are rather than where we think they ought to be.

Stretch forward toward what lies ahead

Just one thing: forgetting what lies behind but straining forward to what lies ahead, I continue my pursuit toward the goal, the prize of God's upward calling, in Christ Jesus. **PHILIPPIANS 3:13–14**

My husband, Ron, brings Paul's metaphor home to me in a very real way. As a longtime runner, Ron keeps looking ahead and not behind. He does so not just for a single race but for all of them. If he has a bad run or disappointing race, he doesn't dwell on it but stretches toward the next one. There is hope embedded in such a view. While the past few years have taken a huge toll on persons and communities around the world, we cannot afford to become mired in the past. Instead, we look ahead to what is to come.

The great Jesuit theologian and paleontologist Teilhard de Chardin wrote that evolution does not depend on a "push from below" but rather on a "pull from above." This is what he identified as the Omega Point. "God, in all that is most living and incarnate in him is not far away from us, altogether apart from the world we see, touch, hear, smell and taste about us. Rather [God] awaits us every instant in our action, in the work of the moment" (*The Divine Milieu*).

While writing the booklet *The Holiness of the Catechist*, I was taken with the number of times the word "beauty" is mentioned in the *Directory for Catechesis*. In paragraph 107, there is a description of the "beautiful words and actions" of Jesus as he healed both physical and emotional wounds and opened hearts to the abundance of God's love. In following the way of Christ, catechists are called to mimic this way of beauty. "The Church, therefore, bears in mind that in order to reach the human heart the proclamation of the Risen One must shine forth with good-ness, truth, and beauty. In this sense, it is necessary 'that every form of catechesis [...] attend to the 'way of beauty'" (108). In attending to this way of beauty, we move forward in hope as well as joy, awakened and stretched by the beauty of God's pres-ence all around us.

<hr>

FOR REFLECTION OR DISCUSSION

How do you see yourself as a hopeful agent of change?
What hope do you hold for the future of catechesis?

The Joy of Catechesis

"Blessed are those..."

So begins each of the Beatitudes as named in Matthew's gospel. Some translations, particularly in Luke's gospel, use the word "happy" instead of blessed. It is a bit jarring when placed in juxtaposition with states of mourning, persecution, and poverty. In contemporary parlance, happiness means bliss and the absence of misery, uncertainty, stress, and dis-ease. The Beatitudes certainly don't guarantee that kind of happy life. Instead, they promise grace that emerges from even the most heartrending circumstances. As such, the Beatitudes are a profound profession of hope. Might they also be invitations to great joy? If so, we might look at how we bring the message of blessing and joy forward.

We might start with considering whether the news we as Christians carry to the world is actually *good*. At times in our history, we went overboard with a gloomy message about the burdens of discipleship. At other times, we made the Christian life into a kind of Disneyland for believers and the gospel into something "nice." Worst of all is when we reduce the faith into something mediocre and mundane. Platitudes replace passion, and our responses to those startling liturgical statements—*"The Lord be with you!" "The word of the Lord!" "The Body of Christ!"*—become rote and mindless.

As part of the call to accompany others in their faith, Pope Francis emphasizes the need to do so with joy. In *Evangelii Gaudium*, he reminds us of the place of happiness and joy in the process of evangelization: "[Christians] should appear as people who wish to share their joy, who point to a horizon of beauty and who invite others to a delicious banquet. It is not by proselytizing that the Church grows, but 'by attraction'" (14). Catechists invite others to see and hear and open their minds and hearts to truly good news. In doing so, where do we find joy in sharing the Good News? How do we witness to others what it means to be committed to Christ?

Bill Miller drew attention to these and other questions as he emphasized the need for joy in moving forward in our catechetical efforts. (See Appendix 2 for excerpts on joy taken from his book *Finding Your Spiritual Direction as a Catechist*.)

Such emphasis meshes with the *Directory*'s description of the kerygmatic nature of evangelization—one that is "marked by joy, encouragement, liveliness, and a harmonious balance which will not reduce preaching to a few doctrines" (59).

We have only to draw upon figures from the gospels to see how this works. Those who heard the words and felt the touch of Jesus as he preached, healed, and restored dignity in those cast aside by societal and religious norms of the day. Each was touched in a deep and personal way and was then compelled to take what they had experienced to others. The words of the Emmaus disciples encapsulate this zeal: "Were not our hearts burning [within us] while he spoke to us on the way and opened the scriptures to us?" (Luke 24:32). What kind of fire burns within us as we retell the gospel stories, as we explore questions of faith, as we witness to the ways God's love has moved in our lives?

In naming the Beatitudes as "the identity card" of the Christian, the *Directory* describes the work of catechesis in dynamic terms: "Catechesis has the task of making the heart of every Christian resound with the call to live a new life in keeping with the dignity of children of God received in Baptism and with the life of the Risen One that is communicated through the sacraments" (83). Note the reference to "resound with the call to live a new life." The catechetical task is no dry recitation of creedal statements or rote memorization of texts that hold little relevance to contemporary realities. Rather, it is one that is infused with the joy of the gospel and enflamed with hope for the present and into the future.

Which of the Beatitudes do you consider your "identity card"?
Where do you find joy in the ministry of catechesis?

Moving Forward

See, I am doing something new! Now it springs forth, do you not perceive it? In the wilderness I make a way, in the wasteland, rivers.
ISAIAH 43:19

I started chapter 1 with a recollection of the massive changes that occurred in rapid succession after the onset of the pandemic. After an aborted trip to Florida and an extended stay with my daughter and her family, life unfolded in new and surprising ways. Amid the restrictions imposed by Covid-19, Ron and I welcomed a new grandson and entered a routine of care for him along with his older sister. We managed to sell our home in Castle Rock and settle into a new one where we have more time and space to ourselves while also enjoying the proximity of family. I received numerous invitations to speak to catechists, Catholic school teachers and administrators, catechetical and pastoral leaders, parents, and other groups while ensconced in my home office. I was given time to facilitate a series of inspiring webinars and to write this book. In short, I experienced first-hand a way out of the wasteland that comprised so much of the pandemic.

Others have not been so fortunate. Even as we move toward an endemic in place of a pandemic, human suffering continues in various ways. It makes the who, what, and how of catechesis even more vital. We have much to do. The conclusion of the *Directory for Catechesis* offers an encouraging and inspiring message for shaping the future of catechesis together. "The ability to work together with [Jesus Christ], in addition to consoling, reassuring, and strengthening one in hope, is a cause of great joy, because the Lord of all creation has chosen to share his work with his creatures" (427). As we move forward together, let us take heart in this assurance of Christ's eternal presence, guidance, and love.

May the God of hope fill you with all joy and peace in believing, so that you may abound in hope by the power of the holy Spirit. ROMANS 15:13

APPENDIX 1

Bill Miller, "Going Backward to Go Forward"

EXCERPTS FROM *ON CHRISTIAN HOPE (SPE SALVI)* BY POPE BENEDICT XVI

(Available through the Vatican website and from the United States Conference of Catholic Bishops)

The realization that there is One who even in death accompanies me, and with his "rod and his staff comforts me," so that I "fear no evil" (cf. Ps 23 [22]:4)—this was the new hope that arose over the life of believers. **(6)**

This is how Jesus expresses it in Saint John's gospel: "I will see you again and your hearts will rejoice, and no one will take your joy from you" (16:22). **(12)**

This is what it means to say: Jesus Christ has "redeemed" us. Through him we have become certain of God... because his only begotten Son has become man and of him everyone can say: "I live by faith in the Son of God, who loved me and gave himself for me" (Gal 2:20). **(26)**

We need the greater and lesser hopes that keep us going day by day. But these are not enough without the great hope, which must surpass everything else. This great hope can only be God, who encompasses the whole of reality and can bestow upon us what we, by ourselves, cannot attain. **(31)**

St. Augustine preached that human beings yearn for God, but our hearts must be constantly stretched and purified in order to begin to experience the divine. His metaphorical example is brilliant:

"Suppose that God wants to fill you with honey [a symbol of God's tenderness and goodness]; but if you are full of vinegar, where will you put the honey?" The vessel, that is your heart, must first be enlarged and then cleansed, freed from vinegar and its taste. This requires hard work and is painful, but in this way alone do we become suited to that for which we are destined. **(33)**

Hope in a Christian sense is always hope for others as well....It is an active hope also in the sense that we keep the world open to God. Only in this way does it continue to be a truly human hope. **(34)**

It is important to know that I can always continue to hope, even if in my own life, or the historical period in which I am living, there seems to be nothing left to hope for. Only the great certitude of hope that my own life and history...are held firm by the indestructible power of Love, and that this gives them their meaning and purpose, only this kind of hope can then give the courage to act and to persevere. **(35)**

The capacity to suffer for the sake of the truth is the measure of humanity. Yet this capacity to suffer depends on the type and extent of the hope that we bear within us and build upon. **(39)**

In this beautiful prayer to Mary, the Mother of God, Pope Benedict shows his gratitude to her for being the "Star of Hope":

Holy Mary, you belonged to the humble and great souls of Israel....Your life was thoroughly imbued with the scriptures of Israel which spoke of hope, of the promise made to Abraham and his descendants (cf. Lk 1:55)....Through you, through your "yes," the hope of the ages became reality, entering this world and its history. When you hastened with holy joy across the mountains of Judea to see your cousin Elizabeth, you became the image of the Church to come, which carries the hope of the world in her womb across the mountains of history. (50)

Thus you remain in the midst of the disciples as their Mother, as the Mother of hope. Holy Mary, Mother of God, our Mother, teach us to believe, to hope, to love with you. (50)

APPENDIX 2

Bill Miller, "Going Backward to Go Forward"

ON JOY: EXCERPTS FROM *FINDING YOUR SPIRITUAL DIRECTION AS A CATECHIST*
BY WILLIAM B. MILLER

(Available from Twenty-Third Publications and from the author's website)

When we begin to see God as the one who will never abandon us, who is our biggest fan, the only one who can and does love us without conditions or restrictions, we are set to begin the experience of a lifetime, the experience of feeling pure joy. **(P. 6)**

Pope Francis reminds us: "The joy of the Gospel is such that it cannot be taken away from us by anyone or anything (cf. Jn 16–22)....One of the more serious temptations which stifles boldness and zeal is the defeatism which turns us into querulous and disillusioned pessimists, 'sourpusses.'"

(FROM *EVANGELII GAUDIUM*, P. 7)

What often draws others to us...is the quality of the joy that can only come from living a life in harmony with the Spirit of God. Moreover, that same quality is what keeps people, whether they are our friends or those we are helping to form in our catechetical sessions, coming back. **(P. 7)**

Deep and abiding love, as may be found in the relationship one develops with the Lord, should inspire great joy! Moreover, it is an exquisite invitation for others to "come and see" what the Lord has for them—that is: love beyond all comprehension and joy beyond all measure. **(P. 7)**

When our daughter, Laura, was in high school, she participated in a two-week mission trip to the Dominican Republic. In many ways, it was a life changing experience for her. When I asked her to name her most profound "learning" from the trip she said, almost without hesitation: "I was amazed by how joyful the people were.

They didn't have all the fancy stuff we have in the United States, but they had strong faith-filled families. They looked out for one another and cared for one another. They were very happy, and they welcomed us with open arms." **(P. 8)**

Presbyterian Minister Frederick Buechner, speaking about making significant life decisions, has said: "The place God calls you to is the place where your deep gladness and the world's deep hunger meet." **(P. 9)**

In the movie *Chariots of Fire*, Olympic medalist Eric Liddell is asked why he loves to run. His reply is both spiritual and profoundly joyful: "When I run, I feel God's pleasure." **(P. 10)**

We must attract them by joy in order to lead them to its source, the Heart of Christ (St. Katharine Drexel). **(P.10)**

A cheerful heart is good medicine, but a downcast spirit dries up the bones (Proverbs 17:22). **(P. 10)**

Recall a time when you felt great joy connected with some aspect of your spiritual life. Pause to remember as many details about the experience as possible. What do you think contributed to the joy you felt? If comfortable doing so, share this story with someone. **(P. 11)**

Have you ever met someone who radiates the joy of the Lord? What do you feel when you are in the presence of that person? If you desired to become more like that person, what do you think you would have to do? **(P. 11)**

APPENDIX 3

Connie Clark, "Family Connections"

Guided Conversations: A Brief Outline

A guided conversation is a strategy that provides a framework for conversation and sharing. We can use it in catechesis to draw families into conversations about their experiences, especially in light of the pandemic. The intention is to guide families toward seeing their experiences in the light of Christ's love.

A guided conversation can happen within the context of an online or in-person meeting, or the individual questions can be sent home as exercises to do as a family. (If sent home as part of family faith formation materials packet, try to provide time and space for some sort of family sharing with others in the community.)

Inviting Families to Participate: The Language of Invitation

Whether you send out formal invitations to an event or you simply ask parents to participate at home, make sure to keep the language inviting:

- We gather as a family in Christ.
- We can laugh, cry, and share together.
- What have you learned that you don't want to forget from these pandemic times? What do you want to share with your children and your community about it?

Prepare: Keep it Simple

- Have people find a touchstone or tactile item from the pandemic to jog their memory.
- Make sure to provide writing materials. If you are sending home questions, encourage families to write down their answers and save them.

The Beatitudes: Our Guide for Conversation

Blessed are the poor in spirit,
    for theirs is the kingdom of heaven.
Blessed are they who mourn,
    for they will be comforted.
Blessed are the meek,
    for they will inherit the land.
Blessed are they who hunger and thirst for righteousness,
    for they will be satisfied.

Blessed are the merciful,
  for they will be shown mercy.
Blessed are the clean of heart,
  for they will see God.
Blessed are the peacemakers,
  for they will be called children of God.
Blessed are they who are persecuted for the sake of
  righteousness,
    for theirs is the kingdom of heaven.
Blessed are you when they insult you and persecute you and
  utter every kind of evil against you [falsely] because of me.
Rejoice and be glad, for your reward will be great in heaven.

MATTHEW 5:3–12

Guided Conversation Starters

**1. *Blessed are the poor in spirit, for theirs
is the kingdom of heaven.***

- Where was I poor during the pandemic?
- What did I miss most? How were our family celebrations
  "poor" but truly blessed?
- When was I afraid?
- Where was my understanding "poor"? (Were there events
  or people I underestimated? When and how did that
  change?)
- Action item: *Whom do I need to thank?*

2. *Blessed are they who mourn, for they will be comforted.*

- Whom or what did I mourn?
- What is a mistake I made that I mourn? (Probably best for silent meditation)
- Who comforted me? Whom did I comfort?
- Where and when did I see my children comforting someone?
- Action item: *What do I want to say to God about this?*

3. *Blessed are the meek, for they will inherit the land.*

- When did I have to bite my tongue? (Positive or negative experience?)
- When did I resist God or what God was saying to me? (Best for silent meditation, or maybe not!)
- Name a strength you/your child discovered that you did not know you had.
- Action item: *How can I or my child use this strength for our family? For others? For the Church?*

4. *Blessed are they who hunger and thirst for righteousness, for they will be satisfied.*

- Where did I see a lack of love—perhaps too close to home?
- When did my family hunger for something? How did we respond?
- When did I find a moment of unexpected grace?
- Action item: *Evaluate my support structures: Where am I getting support? Where do I need it?*

5. Blessed are the merciful, for they will be shown mercy.

- When did I/my child need the "mercy" of some space (physical or emotional)? What was that like?
- How did I provide space for my family? For others?
- Where did I see mercy in action that truly moved me?
- Who reached out to me in mercy?
- Action item: *Who needs my mercy right now? I ask God for help.*

Things to think about:

How might a guided conversation look and sound for the families in your community?

> The Synod then offers us the opportunity to become a listening Church, to break out of our routine and pause from our pastoral concerns in order to stop and listen... to our brothers and sisters speak of their hopes and of the crises of faith present in different parts of the world, of the need for a renewed pastoral life and of the signals we are receiving from those on the ground. **POPE FRANCIS, FROM HIS ADDRESS FOR THE OPENING OF THE SYNOD, OCTOBER 9, 2021**

> Listening is not just useful in helping us to communicate better: It is itself a healing art....Listening is Godly. God spends most of his time listening to our prayers. Prayers are healing because we get to talk, and God listens. **THOMAS REESE, SJ**

RESOURCES

Boyle, Gregory. *Tattoos on the Heart: The Power of Radical Kinship* (Simon and Schuster, 2017)

Clark, Connie. *Make Friends with the Saints* (Twenty-Third Publications, 2019)

Danesco, Lee. *Catechists Awake!* (Twenty-Third Publications, 2021)

Directory for Catechesis. Pontifical Council for the Promotion of the New Evangelization (United States Conference of Catholic Bishops, 2020)

Evangelii Gaudium: The Joy of the Gospel. Pope Francis (The Word Among Us Press, 2013)

Eipers, Carole. *Developing a More Flexible Parish: 8 Easy Ways to Practice Pivoting* (Twenty-Third Publications, 2022)

Halbach, Matthew. *The New Directory for Catechesis: Highlights and Summaries for Catechists and Pastoral Leaders* (Twenty-Third Publications, 2020)

Miller, William. *Finding Your Spiritual Direction as a Catechist* (Twenty-Third Publications, 2017)

Palmer, Parker. *Let Your Life Speak* (Jossey-Bass, 2000)

Powers, William. *Hamlet's BlackBerry: Building a Good Life in the Digital Age* (Harper Perennial, 2011)

Radtke, Barbara. *Understanding the Sacraments* (Twenty-Third Publications, 2018)

Rausch, Thomas P. *I Believe in God* (Liturgical Press, 2008)

Refresh Your Faith series (Twenty-Third Publications, 2020) Clark, Connie. *The Witness of Faith in the Home;* Eipers, Carole. *The Scope and Tasks of Catechesis;* Hendricks, Kathy. *The Holiness of the Catechist;* Schaeffler, Janet. *The Gift of Being a Catechist*

Rolheiser, Ronald. *The Holy Longing* (Doubleday, 1999)

Rohr, Richard. *The Divine Dance* (Whitaker House, 2016)

Schaeffler, Janet. *The Creed: A Catechist's Guide* (Twenty-Third Publications, 2014)

Schut, Michael, ed. *Simpler Living, Compassionate Life* (Church Publishing, 1999)

Steindl-Rast, David. *Commonsense Spirituality* (Crossroad, 2008)

"Still Blooming," blog by Barbara Radtke and Kathy Hendricks, stillblooming.blog

Utter, Denise. *Engage Every Family: A Parish Guide to Integrated Faith Formation* (Twenty-Third Publications, 2022)